Mastering JavaFX 10

Build advanced and visually stunning Java applications

Sergey Grinev

BIRMINGHAM - MUMBAI

Mastering JavaFX 10

Copyright © 2018 Packt Publishing

Commissioning Editor: Amarabha Banerjee
Acquisition Editor: Denim Pinto
Content Development Editor: Gauri Pradhan
Technical Editor: Rutuja Vaze
Copy Editor: Safis Editing
Project Coordinator: Sheejal Shah
Proofreader: Safis Editing
Indexer: Tejal Daruwale Soni
Graphics: Jason Monteiro
Production Coordinator: Shantanu Zagade

First published: May 2018

Production reference: 1290518

Published by Packt Publishing Ltd.
Livery Place
35 Livery Street
Birmingham
B3 2PB, UK.

ISBN 978-1-78829-382-2

www.packtpub.com

To my mom, Raisa, and my wife, Irina, without whom this book would have never happened. To my son, Alexander, who'll learn to read way after this book becomes obsolete.

`mapt.io`

Mapt is an online digital library that gives you full access to over 5,000 books and videos, as well as industry leading tools to help you plan your personal development and advance your career. For more information, please visit our website.

Why subscribe?

- Spend less time learning and more time coding with practical eBooks and Videos from over 4,000 industry professionals

- Improve your learning with Skill Plans built especially for you

- Get a free eBook or video every month

- Mapt is fully searchable

- Copy and paste, print, and bookmark content

PacktPub.com

Did you know that Packt offers eBook versions of every book published, with PDF and ePub files available? You can upgrade to the eBook version at `www.PacktPub.com` and as a print book customer, you are entitled to a discount on the eBook copy. Get in touch with us at `service@packtpub.com` for more details.

At `www.PacktPub.com`, you can also read a collection of free technical articles, sign up for a range of free newsletters, and receive exclusive discounts and offers on Packt books and eBooks.

Contributors

About the author

Sergey Grinev is an experienced software engineer focused on building reliable, quality processes for Java platforms. He started working in this area during his employment with Oracle, where he was responsible for JavaFX testing. For the last few years, Sergey has worked for Azul Systems, assuring the quality of their custom JVMs.

Sergey enjoys sharing his experience: he regularly presents Java conferences, gives lessons, and solves questions on Stack Overflow.

Writing a book is way harder than I thought, and I'm deeply grateful to the people who helped me.

Thanks to my mother, Raisa, who made me study English from the age of 5.
Thanks to my beloved family, Irina and Alexander, for always inspiring me and coping with a half-absent father.

Thanks to my English teacher and friend, April, for the support and inspiration.

Also, great thanks to my editor, Gauri, and the whole Packt team.

About the reviewer

Naman Nigam is a philomath currently working as a software developer with Flipkart. He is heavily involved in gamification and personalization platforms to develop services and features that are responsible for customer engagement at Flipkart. He keeps up to date with the technological upgrades available and their usages, while helping with code reviews, ensuring a consistent performance alongside.

The Flipkart tech team has been extremely helpful during the review process by providing environments where Naman was able to experiment with some of the latest Java releases.

I would like to thank my wife, Neha, who stood by me heedfully whenever I'd take out some time reviewing the book, and my friends who persistently encouraged me to be a part of it.

Packt is searching for authors like you

If you're interested in becoming an author for Packt, please visit authors.packtpub.com and apply today. We have worked with thousands of developers and tech professionals, just like you, to help them share their insight with the global tech community. You can make a general application, apply for a specific hot topic that we are recruiting an author for, or submit your own idea.

Table of Contents

Preface

JavaFX is a set of libraries added to Java in order to provide capabilities to build a modern UI. It was added to Java a few releases ago, as old libraries—Swing and AWT—proved to be outdated and too burdened with backward compatibility issues.

JavaFX was designed and developed from scratch to provide Java developers with the capabilities to build modern, rich UI applications with a large set of shapes, controls, and charts. It was designed with performance in mind, is capable of using graphics cards, and is based on the new graphical engine.

In this book, we will study many aspects of JavaFX and go through a large set of examples based on these topics.

Who this book is for

Developers who already use Java and want to add JavaFX to their skill set, students who study Java or computer science and want to use JavaFX to improve their projects, programmers familiar with JavaFX who want to enrich their experience and learn about the new features of the JavaFX 9 and 10 releases.

What this book covers

Chapter 1, *Stages, Scenes, and Layout*, starts from the essential basis of the JavaFX application—Stage, Scene, JavaFX Event Thread, and the layout graph concept.

Chapter 2, *Building Blocks – Shapes, Text, and Controls*, fills the window we created in the previous chapter with various building blocks provided by the JavaFX API.

Chapter 3, *Connecting Pieces – Binding*, explains that binding is a new method to greatly simplify communication between components.

Chapter 4, *FXML*, introduces FXML is a powerful tool for building a complex JavaFX UI and separating business logic from UI design. We will design an FXML application and try SceneBuilder—an FXML-based UI designer tool.

Chapter 5, *Animation*, demonstrates how to use the JavaFX Animation API to create various types of dynamic content.

Chapter 6, *Styling Applications with CSS*, outlines that JavaFX supports **Cascading Style Sheets** (**CSS**) to style applications similar to web pages.

Chapter 7, *Building a Dynamic UI*, reviews several JavaFX practices to build a modern adaptive UI.

Chapter 8, *Effects*, explains that effects such as a reflection or shadow are an essential part of modern applications.

Chapter 9, *Media and WebView*, showcases how JavaFX provides special controls dedicated to video, audio, and web content.

Chapter 10, *Advanced Controls and Charts*, reviews complex controls such as tables and charts.

Chapter 11, *Packaging with Java9 Jigsaw*, goes through the next step after writing an application—deploying it to end users. We will review JavaFX app building, packaging, and Jigsaw modularization options.

Chapter 12, *3D at a Glance*, teaches us to create several small 3D applications and study JavaFX's 3D capabilities.

Chapter 13, *What's Next?*, looks at further options for mastering JavaFX.

To get the most out of this book

I hope you agree that we really need to write actual code to study programming. This book is built around code samples. Every section in the book is accompanied by a corresponding code sample and, if applicable, screenshots.

Before starting to read this book, I strongly encourage you to get a Git and download the accompanying GitHub repository, which you can find at https://github.com/sgrinev/mastering-javafx-9-10-book.

There are about 130 code samples, grouped by chapters numbers. For your convenience, each chapter is a NetBeans project, but almost every code sample is self-sufficient and can be run separately without the help of an IDE. If you opt for the latter approach, you can find the guidelines for running JavaFX apps from the command line in Chapter 11, *Packaging with Java9 Jigsaw*.

At the time of writing, you need the latest in-development version of Netbeans to work with Java 9 and 10. You can find it at `http://bits.netbeans.org/download/trunk/nightly/latest/`.

While you can get a good grasp of the topics described by just reading the book and looking at the screenshots, toying with the code samples and seeing the results of your changes will give you a much better understanding of JavaFX APIs.

Also, although the book has been released once and for all, I plan to update and fix these samples if any issues are found later on. Refer to GitHub's `README.md` for a history of changes.

Download the example code files

You can download the example code files for this book from your account at `www.packtpub.com`. If you purchased this book elsewhere, you can visit `www.packtpub.com/support` and register to have the files emailed directly to you.

You can download the code files by following these steps:

1. Log in or register at `www.packtpub.com`.
2. Select the **SUPPORT** tab.
3. Click on **Code Downloads & Errata**.
4. Enter the name of the book in the **Search** box and follow the onscreen instructions.

Once the file is downloaded, please make sure that you unzip or extract the folder using the latest version of:

- WinRAR/7-Zip for Windows
- Zipeg/iZip/UnRarX for Mac
- 7-Zip/PeaZip for Linux

The code bundle for the book is also hosted on GitHub at `https://github.com/PacktPublishing/Mastering-JavaFX-10`. In case there's an update to the code, it will be updated on the existing GitHub repository.

We also have other code bundles from our rich catalog of books and videos available at `https://github.com/PacktPublishing/`. Check them out!

Download the color images

We also provide a PDF file that has color images of the screenshots/diagrams used in this book. You can download it here: https://www.packtpub.com/sites/default/files/downloads/MasteringJavaFX10_ColorImages.pdf

Conventions used

There are a number of text conventions used throughout this book.

CodeInText: Indicates code words in text, database table names, folder names, filenames, file extensions, pathnames, dummy URLs, user input, and Twitter handles. Here is an example: "You can import one CSS from another using the @import keyword."

A block of code is set as follows:

```
public static void main(String[] args) {
    // you custom code
    Application.launch(MyApplication.class, args);
}
```

When we wish to draw your attention to a particular part of a code block, the relevant lines or items are set in bold:

```
@DefaultProperty("children")
public class Pane
extends Region
```

Any command-line input or output is written as follows:

```
> javac FXApplication.java
> java FXApplication
```

Bold: Indicates a new term, an important word, or words that you see onscreen. For example, words in menus or dialog boxes appear in the text like this. Here is an example: "For example, we see that the area under the mouse cursor is a **DIV,** as shown in the following screenshot."

Warnings or important notes appear like this.

 Tips and tricks appear like this.

Get in touch

Feedback from our readers is always welcome.

General feedback: Email feedback@packtpub.com and mention the book title in the subject of your message. If you have questions about any aspect of this book, please email us at questions@packtpub.com.

Errata: Although we have taken every care to ensure the accuracy of our content, mistakes do happen. If you have found a mistake in this book, we would be grateful if you would report this to us. Please visit www.packtpub.com/submit-errata, selecting your book, clicking on the Errata Submission Form link, and entering the details.

Piracy: If you come across any illegal copies of our works in any form on the Internet, we would be grateful if you would provide us with the location address or website name. Please contact us at copyright@packtpub.com with a link to the material.

If you are interested in becoming an author: If there is a topic that you have expertise in and you are interested in either writing or contributing to a book, please visit authors.packtpub.com.

Reviews

Please leave a review. Once you have read and used this book, why not leave a review on the site that you purchased it from? Potential readers can then see and use your unbiased opinion to make purchase decisions, we at Packt can understand what you think about our products, and our authors can see your feedback on their book. Thank you!

For more information about Packt, please visit packtpub.com.

Stages, Scenes, and Layout 1

During the last decade, user interfaces have evolved beyond the capabilities of the old Java technologies. Modern users want to work with visually appealing applications and are used to the rich user interfaces brought by Web 2.0 and smartphones.

To address that, JavaFX was envisioned and added to Java a few releases ago. It was created from scratch to avoid any backward compatibility issues, and with a great understanding of the needs of modern user interfaces.

In this book, we will review the most important JavaFX APIs and will look into resolving some of the most common problems that JavaFX developers face, based on my development experience and over 500 questions I've answered in the JavaFX section of `stackoverflow.com`.

In the first chapter, we will start with the backstage of a JavaFX application, including its windows and content area, and see which API is responsible for each of these main building blocks:

- `Application`: This handles the application workflow, initialization, and command-line parameters
- `Stage`: The JavaFX term for the window
- `Scene`: This is the place for the window's content
- SceneGraph: The content of the `Scene`

At the end of the chapter, we will create a clock demo that will demonstrate the concepts from this chapter.

Application and JavaFX subsystems

The very first API, `javafx.application.Application`, represents the program itself. It prepares everything for us to start using JavaFX and is an entry point for all standalone JavaFX applications. It does the following:

- Initializes JavaFX toolkit (subsystems and native libraries required to run JavaFX)
- Starts JavaFX Application Thread (a thread where all UI work happens) and all working threads
- Constructs the `Application` instance (which provides a starting point for your program) and calls the user-overridden methods
- Handles application command line parameters
- Handles all cleanup and shutdown once the application ends

Let's look closely at each of these steps.

Components of the JavaFX toolkit

JavaFX toolkit is the stuff hidden under the hood of the JavaFX. It's a set of native and Java libraries that handles all the complexity of the drawing UI objects, managing events, and working with various hardware. Luckily, they are well-shielded by the API from the user. We will have a brief overview of the major components. It can be useful, for example, during debugging your application; by knowing these component names, you will be able to identify potential problems from stack traces or error messages.

Glass toolkit

This toolkit is responsible for low-level interaction with operating systems. It uses native system calls to manage windows, handle system events, timers, and other components.

Note that Glass is written from scratch; it doesn't use AWT or Swing libraries. So, it's better to not mix old Swing/AWT components and JavaFX ones for the sake of performance.

Prism and Quantum Toolkit

Prism renders things. It was optimized a lot over the course of JavaFX releases. Now, it uses hardware acceleration and software libraries available in the system such as DirectX or OpenGL. Also, Prism renders concurrently and also can render upcoming frames in advance while current frames are being shown, which gives a large performance advantage.

Quantum Toolkit manages the preceding Prism, Glass, and JavaFX API and handles events and rendering threads.

Media

This framework is responsible for video and audio data. In addition to playback functionality, JavaFX Media provides advanced functionality—for example, buffering, seeking, and progressive downloading.

For better performance, Media uses the separate thread, which is synchronized with frames, prepared by Prism, to show/play relevant media data using the correct framerate.

WebView/WebEngine

WebView is a web rendering engine based on the OpenSource WebKit engine, it supports the majority of modern HTML features.

Using WebView, you can incorporate any web resources or even whole sites into your JavaFX applications and integrate them with modern web tools, such as Google Maps.

Working with JavaFX Application Thread

Despite the development of the technology, building a thread-safe UI toolkit is still an enormous challenge due to the complexity of the events and state handling. JavaFX developers decided to follow Swing pattern, and instead of fighting endless deadlocks proclaimed that everything in the UI should be updated from and only from a special thread. It's called **JavaFX Application Thread**.

For simple programs, you don't notice this requirement, as common JavaFX program entry points are already run on this thread.

Once you started adding multithreading to your application, you will need to take care of the thread you use to update the UI. For example, it's a common approach to run a lengthy operation on the separate thread:

```
new Thread(() -> {
    //read myData from file
    root.getChildren().add(new Text(myData));
}).start();
```

This code tries to access JavaFX UI from a common `Thread`, and it will lead to:

```
java.lang.IllegalStateException: Not on FX application thread
```

To address that, you need to wrap your JavaFX code in the next construction:

```
Platform.runLater(() -> {
    root.getChildren().add(new Text("new data"));
});
```

> Note that you can not construct UI objects on JavaFX Application Thread. But, once you have showed them to the user you need to follow the JavaFX UI Thread rule.
>
> Also, note that having one thread for the update UI means that while you run your code on this thread nothing is being updated, and the application looks frozen for the user. So, any long computational, network, or file-handling tasks should be run on a regular thread.

If you need to check in your code which thread you are on, you can use the following API:

```
boolean Platform.isFxApplicationThread();
```

Application class

The most common way to use the JavaFX API is to subclass your application from the `javafx.application.Application` class. There are three overridable methods in there:

- `public void init()`: Overriding this method allows you to run code before the window is created. Usually, this method is used for loading resources, handling command-line parameters, and validating environments. If something is wrong at this stage, you can exit the program with a friendly command-line message without wasting resources on the window's creation.

Note this method is not called on *JavaFX Application Thread,* so you shouldn't construct any objects that are sensitive to it, such as `Stage` or `Scene`.

- `public abstract void start(Stage stage)`: This is the main entry point and the only method that is abstract and has to be overridden. The first window of the application has been already prepared and is passed as a parameter.
- `public void stop()`: This is the last user code called before the application exits. You can free external resources here, update logs, or save the application state.

The following JavaFX code sample shows the workflow for all these methods:

 Note the comment in the first line—it shows the relative location of this code sample in our book's GitHub repository. The same comment will accompany all future code samples, for your convenience.

```java
// chapter1/HelloFX.java
import javafx.application.Application;
import javafx.scene.*;
import javafx.stage.Stage;

public class FXApplication extends Application {

    @Override
    public void init() {
        System.out.println("Before");
    }

    @Override
    public void start(Stage stage) {
        Scene scene = new Scene(new Group(), 300, 250);
        stage.setTitle("Hello World!");
        stage.setScene(scene);
        stage.show();
    }

    public void stop() {
        System.out.println("After");
    }
}
```

Note that you don't need the `main()` method to run JavaFX. For example, this code can be compiled and run from the command line:

```
> javac FXApplication.java
> java FXApplication
```

It shows a small empty window:

Using the Application.launch() method

If you need to have control over the moment JavaFX starts, you can use the `Application.launch()` method:

```
public static void main(String[] args) {
    // you custom code
    Application.launch(MyApplication.class, args);
}
```

Here, `MyApplication` should extend `javafx.application.Application`.

Managing command-line parameters

Unlike the regular Java programs, which receive all parameters in the `main(String[] args)` method, JavaFX provides an extra API to get them: `Application.getParameters()`. Then, you can access them next categories:

- raw format: without any changes

- parsed named pairs: only parameters which were formatted as Java options: --name=value. They will be automatically built into a name-value map.
- unnamed: parameters which didn't fit into the previous category.

Let's compile and run a program with next demo parameters (run these commands from Chapter1/src folder of book's GitHub repository):

```
javac FXParams.java
java FXParams --param1=value1 uparam2 --param3=value3
```

This will run next code, see the corresponding API calls in bold:

```
// FXParams.java
System.out.println("== Raw ==");
getParameters().getRaw().forEach(System.out::println);
System.out.println("== Unnamed ==");
getParameters().getUnnamed().forEach(System.out::println);
System.out.println("== Named ==");
getParameters().getNamed().forEach((p, v) -> { System.out.println(p + "="
+v);});
```

JavaFX will parse these parameters and allocated them into categories:

```
== Raw ==
--param1=value1
uparam
--param3=value 3
== Unnamed ==
uparam
== Named ==
param3=value 3
param1=value1
```

Closing the JavaFX application

Usually, the JavaFX application closes once all of its windows (Stages) are closed.

You can close the application at any moment by calling javafx.application.Platform.exit().

Don't call System.exit() as you may be used to doing in Java programs. By doing that you break the JavaFX application workflow and may not call important logic written in on close handlers such as Application.stop().

If you don't want your application to automatically close, add the following code at the beginning of your program:

```
javafx.application.Platform.setImplicitExit(false);
```

Stage – a JavaFX term for the window

Every UI app needs a window. In JavaFX, the `javafx.stage.Stage` class is responsible for that. The very first stage/windows are prepared for you by Application and your usual entry point for the app is method start, which has `Stage` as a parameter.

If you want to have more windows, just create a new `Stage`:

```
Stage anotherStage = new Stage();
stage2.show();
```

Working with Stage modality options

Modality determines whether events (for example, mouse clicks) will pass to an other application's windows. This is important as you would then need to show the user a modal dialog style window or a warning, which should be interacted with before any other action with the program.

`Stage` supports three options for modality:

- `Modality.NONE`: The new `Stage` won't block any events. This is the default.
- `Modality.APPLICATION_MODAL`: The new `Stage` will block events to all other application's windows.
- `Modality.WINDOW_MODAL`: The new `Stage` will block only events to hierarchy set by `initOwner()` methods.

These options can be set by calling the `Stage.initModality()` method.

The following sample shows how it works. Try to run it and close each window to check events handling, and see the comments inline:

```
// chapter1/FXModality.java
public class FXModality extends Application {

    @Override
    public void start(Stage stage1) {
```

```
    // here we create a regular window
    Scene scene = new Scene(new Group(), 300, 250);
    stage1.setTitle("Main Window");
    stage1.setScene(scene);
    stage1.show();

    // this window doesn't block mouse and keyboard events
    Stage stage2 = new Stage();
    stage2.setTitle("I don't block anything");
    stage2.initModality(Modality.NONE);
    stage2.show();

    // this window blocks everything - you can't interact
    // with other windows while it's open
    Stage stage3 = new Stage();
    stage3.setTitle("I block everything");
    stage3.initModality(Modality.APPLICATION_MODAL);
    stage3.show();

    // this window blocks only interaction with it's owner window
(stage1)
    Stage stage4 = new Stage();
    stage4.setTitle("I block only clicks to main window");
    stage4.initOwner(stage1);
    stage4.initModality(Modality.WINDOW_MODAL);
    stage4.show();
  }
}
```

Using Stage styles

Stage style is the way your window is decorated outside of the Scene.

You can control how Stage will look using StageStyle enum values. It can be passed to the constructor or through the initStyle() method:

```
// chapter1/StageStylesDemo
Stage stage = new Stage(StageStyle.UNDECORATED)
// or
stage.initStyle(StageStyle.TRANSPARENT)
```

See the existing options in the following figure. Note that a Windows screenshot was used here, but decorations will look different on other operating systems because they are a part of the OS user interface and not drawn by Java or JavaFX.

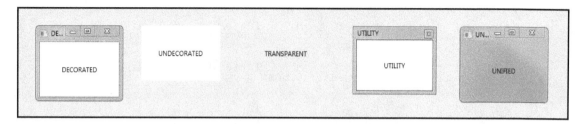

Setting fullscreen and other window options

There are several other options to manipulate `Stage` that are self-explanatory, like in the following examples:

```
// chapter1.StageFullScreen.java
stage.setFullScreen(true);
stage.setIconified(true);
stage.setMaxWidth(100);
//...
```

The only unusual thing about this API is the extra fullscreen options—you can set up a warning message and key combination to exit fullscreen using the following methods:

```
primaryStage.setFullScreenExitHint("Exit code is Ctrl+B");
primaryStage.setFullScreenExitKeyCombination(KeyCombination.valueOf("Ctrl+B
"));
```

Note the convenient `KeyCombination` class, which can parse names of shortcuts. If you prefer more strict methods, you can use `KeyCodeCombination` instead:

```
KeyCodeCombination kc = new KeyCodeCombination(KeyCode.B,
KeyCombination.CONTROL_DOWN);
```

Scene and SceneGraph

Every element of the JavaFX `Scene` is a part of the large graph (or a tree, strictly speaking) that starts from the root element of the `Scene`. All these elements are represented by the class `Node` and its subclasses.

All SceneGraph elements are split into two categories: Node and Parent. Parent is Node as well, but it can have children Node objects. Thus, Node objects are always leaves (endpoints of the SceneGraph), but Parent objects can be both leaves and vertices depending on whether they have children or not.

Parent objects generally have no idea what kind of Node objects their children are. They manage only direct children and delegate all further logic down the graph.

This way, you can build complex interfaces from smaller blocks step by step, organize UI elements in any way, and quickly change the configuration on the higher levels without modifying the lower ones.

Let's take a look at the next short JavaFX application, which shows a window with a checkbox and a gray background:

Take a look at the following code snippet:

```
public class HelloFX extends Application {
    @Override
    public void start(Stage stage) {
        StackPane root = new StackPane();
        CheckBox node = new CheckBox("I'm ready for FX!");
        Rectangle rect = new Rectangle(70, 70, Color.GREEN);
        root.getChildren().addAll(rect, node);
        Scene scene = new Scene(root, 150, 100);
        stage.setScene(scene);
        stage.setTitle("Hello FX!");
        stage.show();
    }
}
```

From the code, the scenegraph here looks like this:

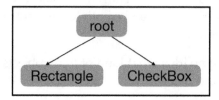

But, `CheckBox` itself consists of several nodes, and by digging deeper you can see that it looks like this:

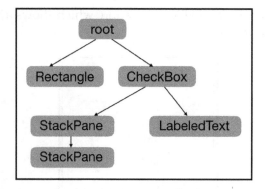

You can always check the scenegraph structure by traversing the graph, starting from the `Scene` root. Here is a convenient method that prints the scenegraph and indents each parent:

```java
public void traverse(Node node, int level) {
  for (int i = 0; i < level; i++) {
    System.out.print(" ");
  }
  System.out.println(node.getClass());
  if (node instanceof Parent) {
    Parent parent = (Parent) node;
    parent.getChildrenUnmodifiable().forEach(n->traverse(n, level +1));
  }
}
```

For our HelloFX example, it will provide the following output:

```
class javafx.scene.layout.StackPane
 class javafx.scene.shape.Rectangle
 class javafx.scene.control.CheckBox
  class com.sun.javafx.scene.control.skin.LabeledText
  class javafx.scene.layout.StackPane
   class javafx.scene.layout.StackPane
```

Organizing the Scene content with Layout Managers

In this section, we will review various Layout Managers that control how your nodes are organized on a `Scene`.

Layout Managers don't have much UI by themselves; usually, only the background and borders are visible and customizable. Their main role is to manage their children nodes.

Free layout

The following managers don't relocate or resize your nodes at all: `Pane`, `Region`, and `Group`. You set coordinates for each of your nodes manually. You can use these layout managers when you want to set absolute positions for each element, or when you want to write your own layout logic.

Let's review the difference between these free layout managers.

The most basic layout manager – Group

`Group` is a very lightweight layout manager. It doesn't support a lot of customizing options (for example, background color) and doesn't have any size control—Group's size is a combination of child sizes, and anything too large will be trimmed.

So, unless you need to have a huge amount of components and care a lot about performance, consider using another manager.

Region and Pane layout managers

Region and Pane support the whole range of styles and effects. They are used as a basis for almost all JavaFX UI components.

The only difference between them is an access level to their children's list.

Pane gives the **public** access to the getChildren() method. So, it's used as an ancestor to layout managers and controls which API allows the manipulating of children.

Region, on the other hand, doesn't allow changing its children list. getChildren() is a private method, so the only way to access them is Region.getChildrenUnmodifiable(), which doesn't allow you to change the list. This approach is used when a component is not meant to have new children. For example, all Controls and Charts extend Region.

Behavioral layout

For these layout managers, you choose the behavior for layouting of your nodes, and they will do the following tasks for you:

- Calculate child nodes' sizes
- Initial positioning of the child nodes
- Reposition nodes if they change their sizes or the layout manager changes its size

The first manager to look at is HBox. It arranges its children in simple rows:

```
HBox root = new HBox(5);
root.getChildren().addAll(
new Rectangle(50, 50, Color.GREEN),
new Rectangle(75, 75, Color.BLUE),
new Rectangle(90, 90, Color.RED));
```

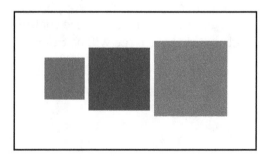

The corresponding VBox does the same for columns.

StackPane positions nodes in its center.

As nodes will overlap here, note that you can control their Z-order using the following APIs:

- Node.toBack() will push it further from the user
- Note.toFront() will bring it to the top position

Take a look at the following example code:

```
Pane root = new StackPane();
Rectangle red;
root.getChildren().addAll(
    new Rectangle(50, 50, Color.GREEN), // stays behind blue and red
    new Rectangle(75, 75, Color.BLUE),
    red = new Rectangle(90, 90, Color.RED));

red.toBack();
```

This is the image that it produces:

Positional layout

This group of managers allows you to choose a more precise location for each component, and they do their best to keep the node there. Each manager provides a distinct way to select where you want to have your component. Let's go through examples and screenshots depicting that.

TilePane and FlowPane

`TilePane` places nodes in the grid of the same-sized tiles. You can set preferable column and row counts, but `TilePane` will rearrange them as space allows.

In the following example, you can see different rectangles being located in the same-sized tiles:

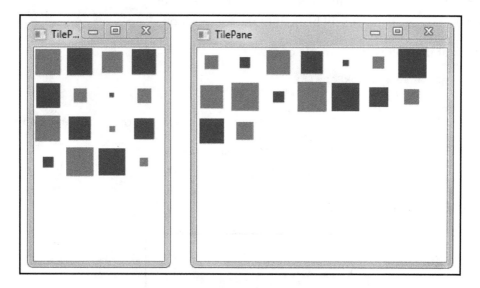

Refer to the following code:

```
// chapter1/layoutmanagers/TilePaneDemo.java
public class TilePaneDemo extends Application {
    @Override
    public void start(Stage primaryStage) {
        TilePane root = new TilePane(5,5);
        root.setPrefColumns(4);
        root.setPrefRows(4);
        // compare to
        // FlowPane root = new FlowPane(5, 5);
        for (int i = 0; i < 4; i++) {
            for (int j = 0; j < 4; j++) {
                double size = 5 + 30 * Math.random();
                Rectangle rect = new Rectangle(size, size,
                        (i+j)%2 == 0 ? Color.RED : Color.BLUE);
                root.getChildren().add(rect);
            }
        }
```

```
        Scene scene = new Scene(root, 300, 250);
        primaryStage.setTitle(root.getClass().getSimpleName());
        primaryStage.setScene(scene);
        primaryStage.show();
    }
}
```

If you don't need tiles to have the same size, you can use `FlowPane` instead. It tries to squeeze as many elements in the line as their sizes allow. The corresponding `FlowPaneDemo.java` code sample differs from the last one only by the layout manager name, and produces the following layout:

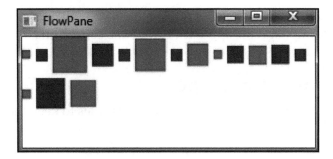

BorderPane layout manager

`BorderPane` suggests several positions to align each subnode: top, bottom, left, right, or center:

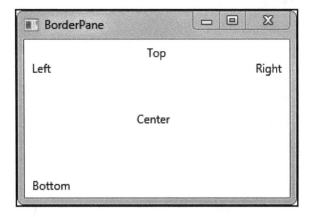

Refer to the following code:

```
BorderPane root = new BorderPane();
root.setRight(new Text("Right "));
root.setCenter(new Text("Center"));
root.setBottom(new Text(" Bottom"));
root.setLeft(new Text(" Left"));

Text top = new Text("Top");
root.setTop(top);

BorderPane.setAlignment(top, Pos.CENTER);
```

Note the last line, where the static method is used to adjust top-element horizontal alignment. This is a JavaFX-specific approach to set Pane **constraints**.

AnchorPane layout manager

This manager allows you to *anchor* any child Node to its sides to keep them in place during resizing:

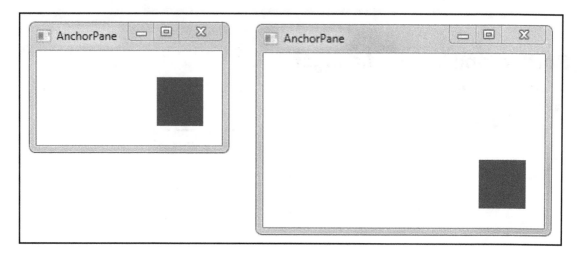

Refer to the following code:

```
Rectangle rect = new Rectangle(50, 50, Color.BLUE);
Pane root = new AnchorPane(rect);
AnchorPane.setRightAnchor(rect, 20.);
AnchorPane.setBottomAnchor(rect, 20.);
```

GridPane layout manager

GridPane is most complex layout manager; it allows users to sets rows and columns where child Nodes can be placed.

You can control a lot of constraints through the API: grow strategy, the relative and absolute sizes of columns and rows, resize policy, and so on. I won't go through all of them to avoid repeating JavaDoc, but will show only a short sample—let's make a small *chessboard pattern* using GridPane:

```
GridPane root = new GridPane();
for (int i = 0; i < 5; i++) {
    root.getColumnConstraints().add(new ColumnConstraints(50));
    root.getRowConstraints().add(new RowConstraints(50));
}
for (int i = 0; i < 5; i++) {
    for (int j = 0; j < 5; j++) {
        if ((i+j)%2 == 0)
            root.add(new Rectangle(30, 30, Color.BLUE), i, j);
    }
}
```

We get the following output:

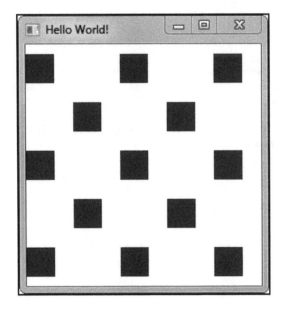

Clock demo

To demonstrate the topics covered in this chapter, I have written a small clock application.

It will become more complex with each upcoming chapter; for the first *release* it just shows a current local time in text form and updates it every second, demonstrating Stage/Scene usage, one of the layout managers, and the Application FX Thread workflow:

See the inline comments for details about the program:

```java
// chapter1/clock/ClockOne.java
public class ClockOne extends Application {
    // we are allowed to create UI objects on non-UI thread
    private final Text txtTime = new Text();
    private volatile boolean enough = false;
    // this is timer thread which will update out time view every second
    Thread timer = new Thread(() -> {
        SimpleDateFormat dt = new SimpleDateFormat("hh:mm:ss");
        while(!enough) {
            try {
                // running "long" operation not on UI thread
                Thread.sleep(1000);
            } catch (InterruptedException ex) {}
            final String time = dt.format(new Date());
            Platform.runLater(()-> {
                // updating live UI object requires JavaFX App Thread
                txtTime.setText(time);
            });
        }
    });
```

```
@Override
public void start(Stage stage) {
    // Layout Manager
    BorderPane root = new BorderPane();
    root.setCenter(txtTime);
    // creating a scene and configuring the stage
    Scene scene = new Scene(root, 200, 150);
    stage.initStyle(StageStyle.UTILITY);
    stage.setScene(scene);
    timer.start();
    stage.show();
}
// stop() method of the Application API
@Override
public void stop() {
    // we need to stop our working thread after closing a window
    // or our program will not exit
    enough = true;
}

public static void main(String[] args) {
    launch(args);
}
}
```

Summary

In this chapter, we studied the main JavaFX concepts: SceneGraph, Application, Stages, and layout. Also, we provided an overview of the main layout managers and wrote our first few JavaFX programs.

A clock demo was presented to demonstrate a JavaFX application lifecycle and working with the threads.

In the next chapter, we'll look into Scene content: Shapes, Text, and basic controls.

Building Blocks – Shapes, Text, and Controls

2

To construct a rich user interface, you need the building blocks. JavaFX provides a large range of very customizable graphical instruments. We'll start from the smallest building blocks—shapes, text, and simple controls—and will use them to understand how JavaFX works with graphical elements.

In this chapter, we will cover the following topics

- Creating and customizing the shapes
- Working with text
- Coordinates and bounds
- Basic controls

By combining and customizing these Nodes and arranging them using the layout managers we reviewed in the previous chapter, you can already build a sophisticated UI. At the end of the chapter, we'll revisit the Clock application from the previous chapter to demonstrate the topics we learned in a more complex application.

Shapes and their properties

Everything you see on the screen of your computer can be split into three large categories:

- Shapes
- Text
- Images

Thus, by being able to create each of these, you can build any UI in reasonable time. Let's start with JavaFX shapes.

JavaFX shapes overview

The simplest object you can put on a scene is a shape. Under the `javafx.scene.shape` `package`, the JavaFX API supports a great range of shapes, from circles and rectangles to polygons and SVG paths. Most shapes can be divided then into two categories—lines and closed shapes. The properties that are shared among all shapes will be covered in the next section. After, we will review each shape's specific APIs.

Closed shapes

There are just four options here—**Rectangle**, **Circle**, **Ellipse**, and **Polygon**. They mostly don't have any special API, just a minimum required by basic math to describe their form.

The only small difference is Rectangle, which can have rounded corners, controlled by the `setArcHeight()` and `setArcWidth()` methods.

For the polygon, you need to provide the coordinates of each vertex through the `getPoints()` method.

For example, take a look at the following code:

```java
// chapter2/shapes/ClosedShapes.java
Rectangle rect = new Rectangle(50,50);
rect.setArcHeight(10);
rect.setArcWidth(10);
rect.setFill(Color.DARKGREY);

Circle circle = new Circle(50);
circle.setFill(Color.DARKGREY);

Ellipse ellipse = new Ellipse();
ellipse.setRadiusX(60);
ellipse.setRadiusY(40);
ellipse.setFill(Color.DARKGREY);

Polygon polygon = new Polygon();
polygon.setFill(Color.DARKGREY);
polygon.getPoints().addAll(
        0.0, 0.0,
        50.0, 30.0,
        10.0, 60.0);

// adding 4 shapes to the scene
HBox hbox = new HBox(20);
```

```
hbox.setPadding(new Insets(20));
hbox.setAlignment(Pos.CENTER);
hbox.getChildren().addAll(rect, circle, ellipse, polygon);
primaryStage.setScene(new Scene(hbox, 500, 150));
```

You can match all four shapes on this screenshot:

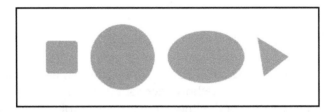

Note that you can have crossing edges for the polygon. JavaFX will do its best to determine which parts of such polygons are internal, judging by the starting point:

```
polygon.getPoints().addAll(
        0., 0.,
        50., 0.,
        0., 50.,
        50., 50.,
        30., -10.,
        20.,70.);
```

The preceding code draws the following shape:

Lines

Line is as simple as it sounds. You write start and end coordinates, and they get connected:

```
Line line = new Line(10, 10, 100, 50);
```

`Polyline` is a set of consecutive lines. You need to provide several pairs of coordinates where the end of each line is the start of the next one. Make sure you are providing an even number of parameters:

```
// chapter2/shapes/Polylines.java
Polyline polyline = new Polyline();
polyline.getPoints().addAll(
        0.0, 0.0,
        50.0, 30.0,
        10.0, 60.0);
```

Note that despite not always having a full border, line-type shapes can have a background. If you assign it using the `setFill()` method, these shapes will use invisible edge, connecting the first and last points of the line. Here is an example of the same polylines with and without a background:

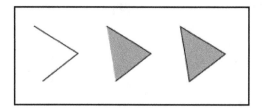

The third shape is a `Polygon` with the same points set. The only difference between `Polygon` and `Polyline` is that the former automatically adds a line between the first and the last points to create a closed figure.

Curves

`Arc` is a piece of the ellipse. It has the extra `startAngle` and `length` properties compared to `Ellipse`. Both these parameters are measured in degrees, ranging from 0 to 360.

The following is an example of an ellipse and a similar arc with a length of 180 degrees:

```
// chapter2/shapes/ArcAndEllipse.java
Ellipse ellipse = new Ellipse();
ellipse.setRadiusX(60);
ellipse.setRadiusY(40);
ellipse.setFill(Color.DARKGREY);

Arc arc = new Arc();
arc.setRadiusX(60);
arc.setRadiusY(40);
```

```
arc.setFill(Color.DARKGREY);
arc.setStartAngle(45);
arc.setLength(180);
```

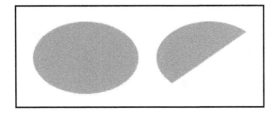

QuadCurve and CubicCurve represent quadratic and cubic Bezier parametric curves. This is a popular method for modeling a smooth curve.

To draw a QuadCurve, you need to set a start point, an end point, and a control point for the curve. After that, JavaFX will draw a curve by shifting tangent with vertexes on the lines from the start point to the control point, and from the control point to the end point.

It's easier than it sounds—luckily, we have a powerful JavaFX API, so I've created a small animation, demonstrating how it works. In the next screenshot, the gray area is a QuadCurve, the two black lines connect the start, end, and control points, and the red line is a moving tangent:

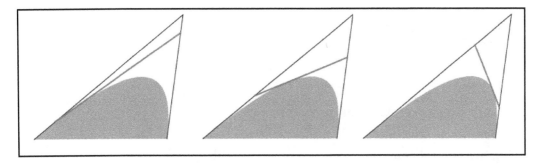

The actual sample is animated, but I'll provide only the curve code for it; see Chapter 5, *Animation*, for the details about the animation API. Take a look at the following code snippet:

```
// chapter2/shapes/AnimatedQuadCurve.java
QuadCurve quad = new QuadCurve();
quad.setStartX(50);
quad.setStartY(200);
quad.setEndX(250);
```

```
quad.setEndY(200);
quad.setControlX(275);
quad.setControlY(20);
quad.setFill(Color.DARKGRAY);

// two lines connecting start, end and control points
Polyline lines = new Polyline(
        quad.getStartX(), quad.getStartY(),
        quad.getControlX(), quad.getControlY(),
        quad.getEndX(), quad.getEndY());

// bold tangent line
Line tangent = new Line(quad.getStartX(), quad.getStartY(),
quad.getControlX(), quad.getControlY());
tangent.setStroke(Color.RED);
tangent.setStrokeWidth(2);
```

CubicCurve is a step up from QuadCurve and has two control points:

```
CubicCurve cubic = new CubicCurve();
cubic.setStartX(50.0);
cubic.setStartY(200.0);
cubic.setControlX1(75.0);
cubic.setControlY1(30.0);
cubic.setControlX2(135.0);
cubic.setControlY2(170.0);
cubic.setEndX(250.0);
cubic.setEndY(190.0);
cubic.setFill(Color.DARKGRAY);

Polyline lines = new Polyline(
        cubic.getStartX(), cubic.getStartY(),
        cubic.getControlX1(), cubic.getControlY1(),
        cubic.getControlX2(), cubic.getControlY2(),
        cubic.getEndX(), cubic.getEndY());
```

By having two control points you can create a shape with an uneven curve:

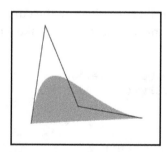

Paths

`Path` is a metashape. You can merge any combination of shape-like `PathElement` objects into one `Path` and use the result as a single shape.

The following `PathElement` classes are supported in JavaFX 9:

`ArcTo`, `ClosePath`, `CubicCurveTo`, `HLineTo`, `LineTo`, `MoveTo`, `QuadCurveTo`, `VLineTo`

Their parameters mostly resemble corresponding shapes, except `ClosePath`, which is a marker of the path end.

Here is an example:

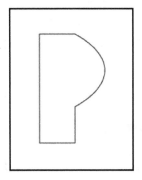

Take a look at the following code snippet:

```
// chapter2/shapes/PathDemo.java
ArcTo arcTo = new ArcTo();
arcTo.setRadiusX(250);
arcTo.setRadiusY(90);
arcTo.setX(50);
arcTo.setY(100);
arcTo.setSweepFlag(true);

Path path = new Path(
        new MoveTo(0, 0),
        new HLineTo(50),
        arcTo, // ArcTo is set separately due to its complexity
        new VLineTo(150),
        new HLineTo(0),
        new ClosePath()
);
```

SVGPath is similar to Path, but it uses text commands instead of code elements. These commands are not specific to JavaFX, they are part of Scalable Vector Graphics specification. So, you can reuse existing SVG shapes in JavaFX:

```
SVGPath svgPath = new SVGPath();
svgPath.setContent("M0,0 H50 A250,90 0 0,1 50,100 V150 H0 Z");
// SVG notation help:
// M - move, H - horizontal line, A - arc
// V - vertical line, Z - close path
svgPath.setFill(Color.DARKGREY);
```

This is the result:

By comparing Path and SVGPath, you can see a certain resemblance. It explains an odd, at first, choice of PathElement objects—they were mimicked after SVG ones.

Adding Text to the JavaFX scene

The last-but-not-least shape to cover is Text. Text draws letters in various fonts. Text weight, posture, and size are controlled by the Font API:

```
// chapter2/other/TextDemo.java
Text txt = new Text("Hello, JavaFX!");
txt.setFont(Font.font ("Courier New", FontWeight.BOLD, FontPosture.ITALIC,
20));
```

Text color is controlled through the standard `setFill()` method, which means we can use all functionality of `Paint` for text as well:

```
// gradient fill, see details few sections below
Stop[] stops = new Stop[]{new Stop(0, Color.BLACK), new Stop(1,
Color.DARKGRAY), new Stop(0.5, Color.ANTIQUEWHITE) };
LinearGradient gradient = new LinearGradient(50, 50, 250, 50, false,
CycleMethod.NO_CYCLE, stops);
txt.setFill(gradient);
```

The output will be as follows:

Text supports multiline strings with a \n delimiter.

For combining different text styles there is the `TextFlow` class, which takes multiple `Text` objects as children:

```
Text txt1 = new Text("Text1");
txt1.setFont(Font.font ("Courier New", 15));
Text txt2 = new Text("Text2");
txt2.setFont(Font.font ("Times New Roman", 20));
Text txt3 = new Text("Text3");
txt3.setFont(Font.font ("Arial", 30));
TextFlow textFlow = new TextFlow(txt1, txt2, txt3);
```

The output is as follows:

Note that `Text` and `TextFlow` support bi-directional text, which will be shown left-to-right when required.

Now we are done with the overview of shapes. Let's look into the common properties all shapes have.

Controlling Shape's color

`Shape` can have two colors: one for the interior (`setFill` method) and one for the border (`setStroke`). Color in JavaFX is handled by the Paint API, which is worth a deeper look:

Paint

Basic paint is just a color. The `Color` class is derived from Paint and provides the following options:

- Predefined constants from `Color.BLACK` to a fancy `Color.ANTIQUEWHITE`
- Color-building methods and corresponding getters—`rgb()`, `hsb()`, `web()`
- Opacity through a parameter of the aforementioned methods
- Color-adjusting methods—`saturate()`, `darker()`, `deriveColor()`, and others

Here is a small example of semi-transparent color circles to show how colors can blend. I understand it's slightly harder to grasp in the black-and-white picture, so try it on your computer:

```
// chapter2/paint/ColorsDemo.java
Pane root = new Pane();
root.getChildren().addAll(
    // RED, opacity 0.3
    new Circle(150,80,70, Color.rgb(255, 0, 0, 0.3)),
    // GREEN, opacity 0.3
    new Circle(100,180,70, Color.hsb(120, 1.0, 1.0, 0.3)),
    // BLUE, opacity 0.3
    new Circle(200,180,70, Color.web("0x0000FF", 0.3))
);
```

The output is as follows:

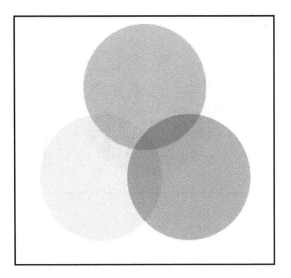

If you want to get rid of color at all, you can use the special constant `Color.TRANSPARENT`.

ImagePattern

`ImagePattern` paint allows us to have an image filling a shape:

```
// chapter2/paint/ImagePatternDemo.java
StackPane root = new StackPane();
root.getChildren().add(
    new Circle(100,
        new ImagePattern(
            new Image(
"https://upload.wikimedia.org/wikipedia/commons/3/3f/Chimpanzee_congo_paint
ing.jpg"
                ))));
```

The output is as follows:

Gradients

Gradients are complex color sequences which change linearly from one to another.

In JavaFX API, each color break is defined by the `Stop` class. Also, by setting coordinates, you can adjust the gradient's direction. For example, in the following code the gradient goes from black to white and from the top-left corner to the bottom-right one:

```
// chapter2/paint/GradientDemo.java
Rectangle rect = new Rectangle(300, 200);
Stop[] stops = new Stop[]{
    new Stop(0, Color.BLACK),
    new Stop(1, Color.ANTIQUEWHITE)};
LinearGradient lg1 = new LinearGradient(0, 0, 300, 200, false,
CycleMethod.NO_CYCLE, stops);
rect.setFill(lg1);
```

Customizing lines with Stroke API

The next `Shape` element is a Stroke—the shape's border. Stroke API governs various attributes of the lines: color, width, location, and dashes.

Basic Stroke

Note that the JavaFX developers decided to not introduce an extra class for strokes; all corresponding methods belong to the `Shape` class instead:

```
shape.setStroke(Color.BLACK);
shape.setStrokeWidth(10);
shape.setStrokeType(StrokeType.CENTERED);
```

The first two are pretty self-explanatory—color and width. Next up is a stroke type that controls positioning relative to shape's edge. See the following image and corresponding sample:

```
// chapter2/strokes/StrokeTypesDemo.java
hbox.getChildren().add(new VBox(5, new Text("NONE"), new Rectangle(50,50,
Color.LIGHTGRAY)));
for (StrokeType type : StrokeType.values()) {
    Rectangle rect = new Rectangle(50,50, Color.LIGHTGRAY);
    rect.setStrokeType(type);
    rect.setStroke(Color.BLACK);
    rect.setStrokeWidth(10);

    hbox.getChildren().add(new VBox(5, new Text(type.toString()), rect));
}
```

We get the following output:

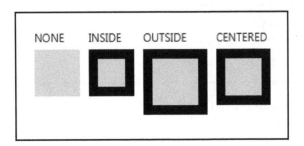

Some shapes may have no inner area at all, for example, `Line`. So, to change the color of such a shape you need to use `setStroke()` rather than `setFill()`.

Dashed lines

By using the `strokeDashArray` method, you can make dashed lines. Each dash's size, and the spaces between them, are set in Stroke Dash Array. Each odd position is the dash length, and each even position is the length of the space before the next dash. Refer to the following code snippet:

```
// chapter2/strokes/DashExamples.java
Line line = new Line(50, 0, 250, 0);
line.setStrokeWidth(10);
line.setStroke(Color.DARKGRAY);
line.getStrokeDashArray().addAll(30.0, 15.0);
```

This method will give us the following line:

Note that the gaps between dashes look smaller than the 15 pixels we set. This is because, by default, `StrokeLineCap` is set to `SQUARE`, which means each gap ends with half of a square shape with a size of the half of stroke width. Here is a comparison of all three line caps:

`line.setStrokeLineCap(StrokeLineCap.SQUARE);`	▬▬ ▬▬ ▬▬ ▬▬ ▬▬
`line.setStrokeLineCap(StrokeLineCap.ROUND);`	▬ ▬ ▬ ▬ ▬
`line.setStrokeLineCap(StrokeLineCap.BUTT);`	▬ ▬ ▬ ▬ ▬

And the last thing to note about dash is offset, which is a point in the dashed line that will be used as a start for drawing it:

```
line.setStrokeDashOffset(20);
```

Connecting line designs using Line Join

Line Join describes how lines will look at intersections or angles. There are several options here:

- `StrokeLineJoin.MITER`: A sharp angle made from outer parts of the connecting lines
- `StrokeLineJoin.BEVEL`: A cut out angle
- `StrokeLineJoin.ROUND`: A rounded-up angle

```
// chapter2.strokes/LineJoins.java
shape.setStrokeLineJoin(StrokeLineJoin.MITER);
shape.setStrokeMiterLimit(3);
```

The output is as follows:

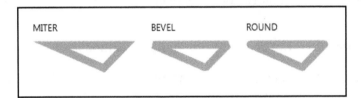

Working with the Shape operations

There are three operations that allow for the combining of two shapes into one:

- **Union**: Combines two shapes
- **Intersect**: Leaves only the shared part of two shapes
- **Subtract**: Removes the shared part from the first shape

These are static methods that can be applied to any two shapes:

```
Circle circle = new Circle(30);
Rectangle rect = new Rectangle(45, 45);
root.getChildren().addAll(
    Shape.union(circle, rect),
    Shape.intersect(circle, rect),
    Shape.subtract(circle, rect));
```

The output is as follows:

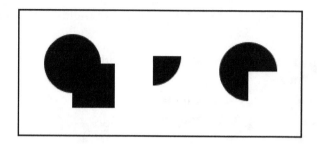

Transformations

JavaFX API supports basic transformations for every Node (and Shape, which extends Node).

Three basic transformations can be used through Node methods:

- setRotate (double angle): Rotates around the center of the Node
- setTranslateX (double pixels), setTranslateY (double pixels): Shifts the Node by a set amount of pixels
- setScaleX (double scale), setScaleY (double scale): Increases (or decreases) the Node by multiplying its horizontal or vertical dimensions by scale

For more complex transformations, the Transform class can be used. It allows us to work precisely with every parameter of the transformation. For example, you can concatenate two transformations into one combined and use two different nodes to save.

Note that through Transform, there are usually more options available. For example, the setRotate() method always uses the center of the shape as a pivot point, whereas for the rotate transformation you can set a deliberate pivot point inside the shape:

```
Rotate rotateTransform = new Rotate();
rotateTransform.setAngle(45);
rotateTransform.setPivotX(10);
rotateTransform.setPivotY(10);
node.getTransforms().add(rotateTransform);
```

The following demo shows rotate, translate, scale, and shear transforms. Additionally, there is a fifth transformation that is a combination of shear and rotate. On the following figure, the black border is an original rectangle and the gray shape is the transformed one:

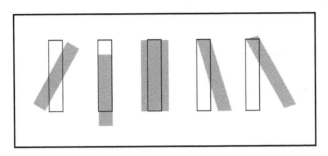

The code for the preceding figure is a bit long because of the *double rectangle* functionality; the actual transformations are at the end. Take a look at the following code snippet:

```java
// chapter2/other/Transformations.java
public class Transformations extends Application {
    // service method to make similar rectangles
    private Rectangle addRect() {
        // here we create two rectangles:
        // one for transformation
        Rectangle rect = new Rectangle(20, 100, Color.DARKGRAY);
        // and another to demonstrate original
        // untransformed rectangle bounds
        Rectangle rectOrig = new Rectangle(20, 100);
        rectOrig.setFill(Color.TRANSPARENT);
        rectOrig.setStroke(Color.BLACK);

        StackPane pane = new StackPane(rect, rectOrig);
        root.getChildren().add(pane);
        return rect;
    }
    TilePane root = new TilePane(50,50);
    @Override
    public void start(Stage primaryStage) {
        // rotate transformation
        Rectangle rect1 = addRect();
        rect1.setRotate(30);
        // translate transformation
        Rectangle rect2 = addRect();
        rect2.setTranslateY(20);
        // scale transformation
        Rectangle rect3 = addRect();
        rect3.setScaleX(2);
```

```
            // shear transformation
            Rectangle rect4 = addRect();
            rect4.getTransforms().add(new Shear(0.3, 0));
            // combining two transformations
            Rectangle rect5 = addRect();
            Transform t1 = new Shear(0.3, 0);
            Transform t2 = new Rotate(-15);
            rect5.getTransforms().add(t1.createConcatenation(t2));
            // adding all transformed rectangles to the scene
            root.setPadding(new Insets(50));
            primaryStage.setTitle("Hello World!");
            primaryStage.setScene(new Scene(root, 500, 250));
            primaryStage.show();
        }
    }
```

Coordinates and bounds

Let's look into determining Shape and Node bounds in Scene and Scenegraph.

The simplest of all are layoutBounds. These rectangular bounds are used for all size and location calculations for this Node, and describe its basic shape size. They don't include any extra effects or transformations.

The next thing is boundsInLocal. These bounds include all information about effects. So, you can determine how large of an area is covered by your Node or Shape.

The last one is boundsInParent. These are bounds after all transformations as well and bounding rectangles uses their parents' coordinate system.

Working with Bounds Demo

There is a very nice public demo by *Kishori Sharan* that shows how bounds work: http://www.java2s.com/Tutorials/Java/JavaFX_How_to/Node/Know_how_three_bounds_layoutBounds_boundsInLocal_and_boundsInParent_are_computed_for_a_node.htm.

It uses a deprecated API, so I've fixed it and added it to our GitHub as chapter2/other/BoundsDemo.java.

In the following screenshot from this demo, there is a Rectangle with rotation and translate transformations, and a shadow effect:

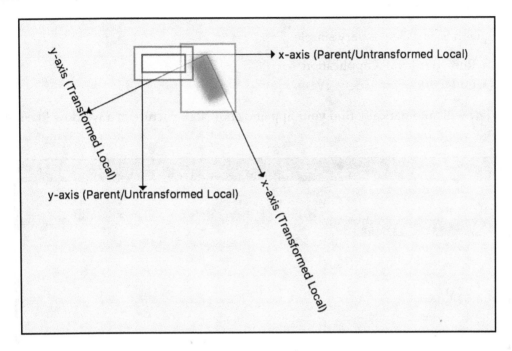

The smallest rectangle represents `layoutBounds`—it's the position of original `Rectangle` before any other changes.

The bigger rectangle around it is `boundsInLocal`—the size of the `Rectangle` after the shadow effect, which spills a bit over the edges.

The blurred rotated rectangle is an actual image you will see after applying all described effects. The large square around it is `boundsInParent`—the actual size the `Rectangle` takes on the `Scene`.

I strongly suggest playing with that demo to get a grasp of how bounds work.

Using the ScenicView tool to study JavaFX scenegraph

ScenicView is a great tool made and supported by one of the JavaFX developers, *Jonathan Giles*. It can be downloaded from `http://fxexperience.com/scenic-view/`.

ScenicView benefits from open JavaFX architecture and the SceneGraph paradigm. It allows the traversing SceneGraph of any JavaFX application to run on the same machine and check the properties of every Node.

Working with ScenicView is very simple:

- Run your JavaFX application
- Call `java -jar scenicView.jar`

ScenicView will automatically find your app and show its structure in a window like the following:

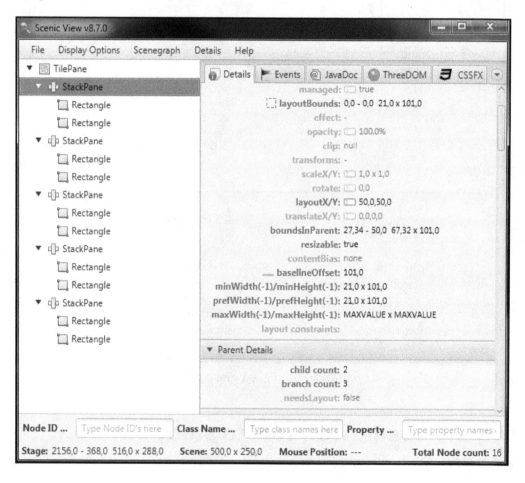

On the left, you can see the scenegraph, and on the right, you can review all properties of the selected node.

Note how the `boundsInParent` and `layoutBounds` properties are additionally marked right inside your application:

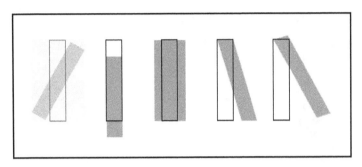

The next feature is **node detection**; by clicking *Ctrl + Shift + S,* ScenicView will detect which node is located at the mouse coordinates, provide a brief description, and select it in the ScenicView on click:

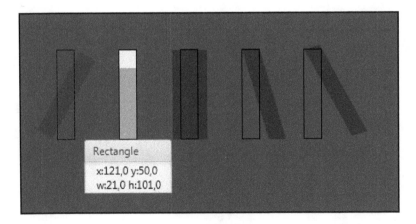

This feature provides immense value while debugging complex JavaFX applications.

Basic Controls

Controls are a special subset of `Node` objects that were designed to handle user interaction. Most of them allow user input and support focus traversal.

Another difference from `Shape` is that `Control` objects are inherited not directly from `Node` but through the `Region` interface (like layout managers), which means their size and location are not fixed and can be managed by layout managers.

Button and Event Handlers

The first and most common control is button's family. `Button` has an `EventHandler` that is called when `Button` is clicked (or fired). All code in the event handler is always run on JavaFX Application Thread:

```
// chapter2/other/ButtonDemo.java
Button btn = new Button();
btn.setText("Say 'Hello World'");
btn.setOnAction(new EventHandler<ActionEvent>() {
    @Override
    public void handle(ActionEvent event) {
        System.out.println("Hello World!");
    }
});
```

In addition to text, you can use any `Node` inside a button:

```
Button btn = new Button();
btn.setText("Say 'Hello World'");
btn.setGraphic(new Circle(10));
```

`Button` can be assigned the roles of default button or cancel button, responding to *Enter* or *Esc* correspondingly:

```
btn.setDefaultButton(true);
//or
btn.setCancelButton(true);
```

`Button` can be easily assigned with a mnemonic *(Alt + letter)* by using the _ sign:

```
btn.setText("_Press Alt+P to fire me."):
```

Note you can disable this behavior by calling `btn.setMnemonicParsing(false);`.

There are also 4 more classes that share a common ancestor (`ButtonBase`) and most functionality with `Button`:

- `ToggleButton` saves state clicked/unclicked and changes visuals accordingly. Its state can be retrieved by calling the `isSelected()` method.
- `CheckBox` has the same behavior as `ToggleButton` but different visuals and API. `CheckBox` state is controlled by the `getState()` method.
- `Hyperlink` is a button with no extra decorations, which also remembers if it was already clicked.
- `MenuButton` is a part of the Menu API that allows you to create user and context menus.

Size of the Controls

`Control` (or any `Region` derived class) has three size limitations:

- `minSize`: Minimal size
- `prefSize`: Preferred size
- `maxSize`: Maximal size

Layout managers, while handling their children, try to use their `prefSize`. If it's not possible, they are obliged to not shrink any child smaller than their `minSize` and not let them grow bigger than their `maxSize`.

Controls usually set their `prefSize` by themselves based on their content.

For example, button prefSize is based on the length of the text inside, `minSize` is just enough to show ellipsis instead of text, and the maxSize of `Button` is similar to `prefSize`.

Thus, you don't need to care about a size of the `Button` in the following sample:

```
VBox root = new VBox(5);
root.setPadding(new Insets(20));
Button btnShort = new Button("short");
btnShort.setMinWidth(50);
root.getChildren().addAll(
        new Button("hi"),
        btnShort,
```

```
                    new Button("mediocre"),
                    new Button("wide-wide-wide")
        );
```

And, if you try to resize the window, the button `btnShort` keeps its width, as shown in the following screenshots:

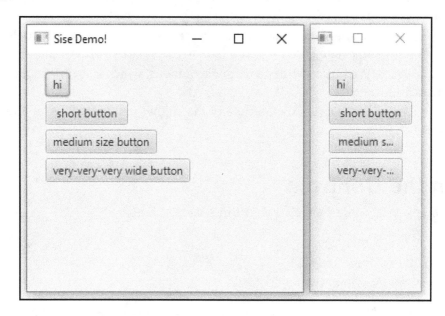

If you want your `Control` or other `Region` to always have a fixed size, you need to set all three sizes to the same value.

> If you want to use Control's own prefSize to be used as max or min you
> can use a special constant—`Control.USE_PREF_SIZE`. For example,
> `btn.setMinHeight(Control.USE_PREF_SIZE);`.

Clock demo

Let's apply some of the stuff we learned in this Chapter to the Clock demo we started in the previous chapter.

The digital clock is not as fun as an analog one, so let's add hands to it.

We need three hands—hours, minutes, and seconds. We'll use a simple line for the seconds hand and slightly more complex path shapes for the hour and minute ones. For example, here is the path for the minute hand:

```
Path minuteHand = new Path(
                new MoveTo(0, 0),
                new LineTo(15, -5),
                new LineTo(100,0),
                new LineTo(15,5),
                new ClosePath());
minuteHand.setFill(Color.DARKGRAY);
```

This code gives us not the prettiest but a conveniently simple hand. We'll work on making it nicer in following chapters:

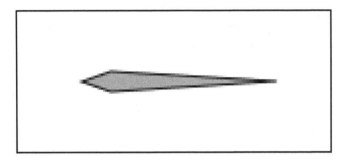

To show time, the hand has to rotate. We'll use the `Rotate` transformation. We need to rotate the hand around the leftmost point, not the center, so we set the pivot point to zero coordinates:

```
Rotate rotateMinutesHand = new Rotate();
rotateMinutesHand.setPivotX(0);
rotateMinutesHand.setPivotY(0);
minuteHand.getTransforms().add(rotateMinutesHand);
```

Now, we can control the time set by modifying the angle for this `Rotate` transformation.

Also, our hand is inside our layout manager, which tries to center it around `Path` central point as well. But, we want to have a center in the local coordinates (0,0). To achieve that, we will translate our hand left by half of its actual size:

```
minuteHand.setTranslateX( minuteHand.getBoundsInLocal().getWidth()/2 );
```

For a better understanding, take a look at the ScenicView screenshot for this code—the dashed box is `layoutBounds` and the colored rectangle is `boundsInParent`, which changes after every rotation:

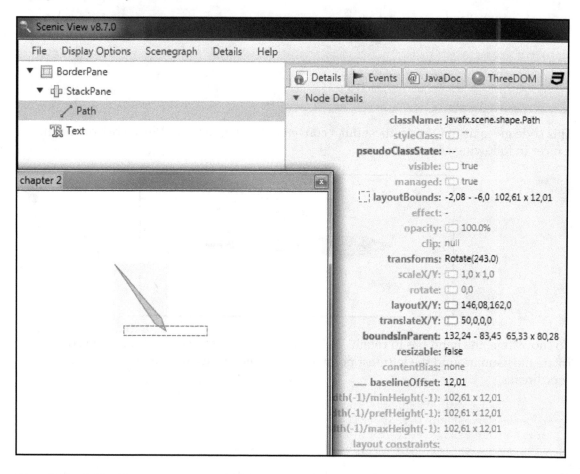

Here is the full code:

```
public class ClockTwo extends Application {
    private final Text txtTime = new Text();

    private Rotate rotateSecondHand = new Rotate(0,0,0);
    private Rotate rotateMinuteHand = new Rotate(0,0,0);
    private Rotate rotateHourHand = new Rotate(0,0,0);
    private Thread timer = new Thread(() -> {
        SimpleDateFormat dt = new SimpleDateFormat("hh:mm:ss");
        Date now = new Date();
```

```
        String time = dt.format(now);
        Platform.runLater(()-> {
                // updating live UI object requires JavaFX App Thread
                rotateSecondHand.setAngle(now.getSeconds() * 6 - 90);
                rotateMinuteHand.setAngle(now.getMinutes()* 6 - 90);
                rotateHourHand.setAngle(now.getHours()* 30 - 90);
                txtTime.setText(time);
        });
        try {
                // running "long" operation not on UI thread
            Thread.sleep(1000);
        } catch (InterruptedException ex) {
        }
    });

    @Override
    public void start(Stage stage) {
        // create minutes hand
        Path minuteHand = new Path(
                new MoveTo(0, 0),
                new LineTo(15, -5),
                new LineTo(100,0),
                new LineTo(15,5),
                new ClosePath());
        minuteHand.setFill(Color.DARKGRAY);
        minuteHand.getTransforms().add(rotateMinuteHand);
minuteHand.setTranslateX(minuteHand.getBoundsInLocal().getWidth()/2);
        // create second hand
        Line secondHand = new Line(0,0, 90, 0);
        secondHand.getTransforms().add(rotateSecondHand);
secondHand.setTranslateX(secondHand.getBoundsInLocal().getWidth()/2);
        // create hour hand
        Path hourHand = new Path(
                new MoveTo(0, 0),
                new LineTo(20, -8),
                new LineTo(60,0),
                new LineTo(20,8),
                new ClosePath());
        hourHand.setFill(Color.LIGHTGRAY);
        hourHand.getTransforms().add(rotateHourHand);
        hourHand.setTranslateX(hourHand.getBoundsInLocal().getWidth()/2);
        BorderPane root = new BorderPane();
        root.setCenter(new StackPane(minuteHand, hourHand, secondHand));
        root.setBottom(txtTime);
        BorderPane.setAlignment(txtTime, Pos.CENTER);
        Scene scene = new Scene(root, 400, 350);
        stage.initStyle(StageStyle.UTILITY);
        stage.setScene(scene);
```

```
        stage.setTitle("Clock, chapter 2");
        timer.setDaemon(true);
        timer.start();
        stage.show();
        System.out.println(minuteHand.getBoundsInLocal().getWidth());
    }
    public static void main(String[] args) {
        launch(args);
    }
}
```

The clock will appear as follows:

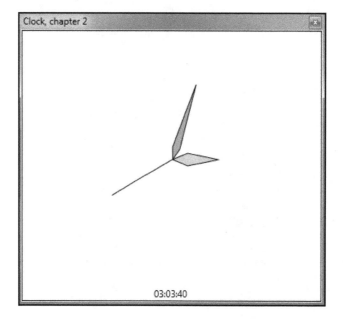

Summary

In this chapter, we've studied a lot of different building blocks for JavaFX applications: shapes, text, and simple controls. Also, we looked at various ways to customize them. With these tools, you can already build a visually rich JavaFX UI.

The only problem is that it will be static, which is not enough for a modern application. In the next two chapters, we will learn about Binding and Animation, which will allow us to develop more dynamic applications.

Connecting Pieces – Binding

3

Dynamically sharing information between UI elements is a big part of an application. We are all used to handling dynamic updates in Java through established means such as listeners or event queues, but JavaFX brought a new option, the Binding API, to directly bind components' properties together.

In this chapter, we will study how the JavaFX Binding API greatly simplifies communication between any JavaFX components—nodes, controls, FX collections, animation, media, and more.

In this chapter, we'll cover the following topics:

- Binding basics and its benefits over regular listeners
- Binding operations
- User-defined or custom bindings
- Binding collections

Working with the Property API

In addition to the regular getters and setters, JavaFX provides a Property API to almost all its classes' fields.

For example, there are the following methods to work with the Stage title:

```
String getTitle();              //getter
void setTitle(String title);    //setter
StringProperty titleProperty(); //property access
```

Technically, getters and setters are not required, and the Property value can be used all the time.

The Property class has the following two important APIs—**Observable** and **Binding**.

Using the Observable API

An `Observable` is an interface which allows you to subscribe to the change event of the corresponding property. All JavaFX properties are observable, thus you can track changes of every small parameter of every JavaFX node using the Observable API.

Let's take a look at the next simple example, which dynamically updates the width of the JavaFX application's window.

The window, represented by the `Stage` class, has a property called `widthProperty`, which we can listen to:

```
// chapter3/basics/WidthObservable.java
public void start(Stage stage) {
    Label lblWidth = new Label();
    // Note, we are not using any binding yet
    stage.widthProperty().addListener(new ChangeListener<Number>() {
      @Override
      public void changed(ObservableValue<? extends Number> o, Number
oldVal, Number newVal) {
               lblWidth.setText(newVal.toString());
            }
    });

    stage.setScene(new Scene(new StackPane(lblWidth), 200, 150));
    stage.show();
}
```

Here is a screenshot:

Every property in JavaFX is implementing the similar `ObservableValue` interface and can be listened to for changes.

Not clearing listeners properly is a common reason for Java memory leaks. To address that, JavaFX supports weak-reference for all listeners, so if you are working on a large application, consider using `WeakListener` descendants and `WeakEventHandler`.

Besides plain values, you can observe collection types through the following interfaces extending `Observable`:

- `ObservableList`: `java.util.List` with the Observable API
- `ObservableMap`: `java.util.Map` with the Observable API
- `ObservableArray`: A class that encapsulates a resizable array and adds the Observable API

Overall, there are over 100 classes implementing `Observable` in JavaFX.

Introducing the Binding API

The Binding API allows you to simplify listeners to just one line of code:

```
// chapter3/basics/WidthBinding.java
public void start(Stage stage) {
    Label lblWidth = new Label();

    lblWidth.textProperty().bind(stage.widthProperty().asString());

    stage.setScene(new Scene(new StackPane(lblWidth), 200, 150));
    stage.show();
}
```

Let's take a closer look at the binding code:

```
lblWidth                // object we want to change
  .textProperty()       // property of the object to be changed
  .bind(                // bind() call
    stage               // object we want to monitor
    .widthProperty()    // property of the monitored object we want to track
    .asString());       // assigning Double value to a String property
```

The bind() method comes from the base Property interface, which has the following API methods:

- bind (ObservableValue<? extends T> observable): Binds a Property to Observable.
- unbind (): Stops binding.
- boolean isBound (): Checks whether a Property is already bound. It's important as only one binding connection can be set for a Property, although this connection can be made as complex as you need, as will be shown later in the chapter.
- bindBidirectional (Property<T> other): Ties two properties together in both directions.
- unbindBidirectional (Property<T> other): Stops the bidirectional binding.

Bidirectional binding connects two properties, essentially making them always have the same value.

Consider the following example:

```java
// chapter3/basics/BidirectionalBindingDemo.java
public void start(Stage stage) {
    Slider s1 = new Slider(0, 100, 40);
    Slider s2 = new Slider(0, 100, 40);
    s2.setOrientation(Orientation.VERTICAL);
    s1.valueProperty().bindBidirectional(s2.valueProperty());

    VBox root = new VBox(5, s1, s2);
    root.setAlignment(Pos.CENTER);
    root.setPadding(new Insets(20));

    stage.setScene(new Scene(root, 200, 150));
    stage.show();
}
```

The preceding code creates two sliders. You can drag either of them and the other one will mimic the movement:

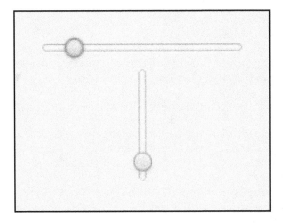

Rules of binding

Although binding looks very simple to use, there are several rules that you need to be aware of while using binding:

- Read-only properties can't be bound
- Only one bind can be active for a property, but several properties can be bound to another one
- Binding and setters do not work together
- Bidirectional bindings are less strict

Let's look at each of these points more closely in the next sections.

Read-only properties

All properties can be observed (or be used as a parameter for bind), but bind can't be called for some of them. The exception is read-only properties, which can't be changed and can't be bound.

All read-only properties implement `ReadOnlyProperty`, or they can be recognized by the class name starting from `ReadOnly` words. For example, `widthProperty` in the first example has the `ReadOnlyDoubleProperty` type.

Binding is a one-to-many relation

Any property can be observed as many times as you want:

```
Label lblWidth = new Label();
Label lblWidth2 = new Label();

lblWidth.textProperty().bind(stage.widthProperty().asString());
lblWidth2.textProperty().bind(stage.widthProperty().asString());
```

But, any consecutive call for the `bind()` method will override the previous one:

```
lblWidth.textProperty().bind(stage.widthProperty().asString());
lblWidth.textProperty().bind(stage.heightProperty().asString());
// now lblWidth listens for height and ignores width
```

Don't be disappointed by this rule. You can call `bind()` effectively only once, right. But, the parameter of `bind()` can be much more complex than just one property. We'll discuss this in more detail in the *Using binding operations* section.

Binding blocks setters

Once a property is bound, you can't set it directly. The following code will throw `RuntimeException: Label.text : A bound value cannot be set`. Take a look at the following code snippet:

```
lblWidth.textProperty().bind(stage.widthProperty().asString());
lblWidth.setText("hi"); // exception
```

If you want to do it, you need to call `unbind()` first.

Bidirectional binding

Bidirectional binding, meanwhile, has much fewer restrictions, because it ties properties harder, so there is no need to extra control them.

You can use setters:

```
label2.textProperty().bindBidirectional(label.textProperty());
label2.setText("hi");
```

You can combine bidirectional and regular bindings:

```
lblWidth.textProperty().bind(stage.widthProperty().asString());
lblWidth2.textProperty().bindBidirectional(lblWidth.textProperty());
```

And, you can bind one property bidirectionally several times:

```
label.textProperty().bindBidirectional(label2.textProperty());
label.textProperty().bindBidirectional(label3.textProperty());
label.setText("hi"); // or label2.setText("hi"); or label3.setText("hi");
                     // any of them will update all three labels at once
```

 Note that the isBound() method works only for one-directional binding. Unfortunately, there is no API to check for bidirectional binding. Also, don't mix unbind(), which works only for regular bindings, and unbindBidirectional(), for bidirectional ones.

Using binding for visual help

While studying JavaFX classes, you can conveniently check how properties work using binding to a slider or checkbox—add them to your program, bind to the property you are interested in, and observe how different values of this property affect the corresponding node.

For example, let's look at this circle and bind a few sliders to its stroke and radius:

```java
// chapter3/basics/CirclePropertiesDemo.java
public void start(Stage primaryStage) {
        Circle circle = new Circle(150, 150, 40, Color.ANTIQUEWHITE);
        circle.setStroke(Color.BLACK);

        Slider sliderRadius = new Slider(0, 100, 40);
        sliderRadius.relocate(80, 20);
        sliderRadius.setShowTickLabels(true);
        sliderRadius.setMajorTickUnit(20);
        circle.radiusProperty()
            .bind(sliderRadius.valueProperty());
        Slider sliderStrokeWidth = new Slider(0, 10, 2);
        sliderStrokeWidth.setShowTickLabels(true);
        sliderStrokeWidth.setMajorTickUnit(2);
        sliderStrokeWidth.relocate(80, 50);
        circle.strokeWidthProperty()
            .bind(sliderStrokeWidth.valueProperty());
        Pane root = new Pane();
        root.getChildren().addAll(sliderRadius, circle, sliderStrokeWidth);
        primaryStage.setTitle("Hello Binding!");
        primaryStage.setScene(new Scene(root, 300, 250));
        primaryStage.show();
    }
```

Here are the examples of this app with sliders moved to different positions:

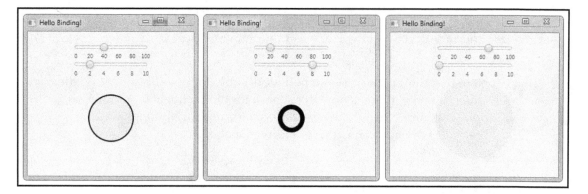

The role of listeners

Note that binding is not a complete replacement for listeners. EventListener objects are still required to program a reaction to the user actions or system events. Binding plays its role, then you need to update one entity based on the state of another.

So, the rule of thumb is, if you are writing ChangeListener or InvalidationListener, consider using binding instead.

Using binding operations

Directly connecting properties is not always enough. The Binding API can build complex dependencies between properties.

String operations

Concatenation is the most common string operation. It's called by one property of the `String` type and takes another property of any type or a constant that will be used as a `String`, as shown in the following code snippet:

```
// chapter3/operations/ConcatBinding.java
label.textProperty().bind(
    stage.widthProperty().asString()  // property one
    .concat(" : ")                    // concatting with a string constant
    .concat(stage.heightProperty())   // concatting with a property 2
);
```

 You don't need to call `asString()` for a `concat()` parameter, as it's done by JavaFX.

Note two very important concepts here:

- Binding operations allow us to chain them one after another (as in the Builder pattern, or in the Java8 Streams API)
- We've bound one property to the two others here

And, we are not limited by two properties: you can build a binding or almost any complexity by chaining method calls.

For strings, most of the binding utility is available in the `StringExpression` class, which allows using string-relevant functions as bindings. `StringExpression` implements `ObservableStringValue` and is an ancestor for `StringBinding`. So, any string-related binding will have it in a chain of inheritance.

For example, if you want to bind to string length, you can use the `StringExpression` method `length()`, which returns an `IntegerBinding` type. Here is an example:

```
// chapter3/operations/StringLengthBind.java
public void start(Stage stage) {
    TextField textField = new TextField();
    Label lblLength = new Label();

    lblLength.textProperty().bind(
        textField.textProperty()
            .length()    // this length returns IntegerBinding, not just an
integer
            .asString() // so you can keep observing it and use binding
```

```
methods
      );

    HBox root = new HBox(20, textField, lblLength);
    root.setAlignment(Pos.CENTER);
    stage.setScene(new Scene(root, 200, 100));
    stage.show();
}
```

And, this code gives us an automatic length counter for a text field, as shown in the following screenshot:

For even more flexibility, you can use the `Bindings` utility class, which holds quite a few utility methods. Even the preceding `concat()` method was added only for convenience and is implemented through calls to `Bindings`.

For example, it would be convenient to have the word `"Count:"` shown in front of the number. But, how one can add a String before a bindable object? There is nothing to call `concat()` from yet. `Bindings` comes to help here with the static `concat()` method:

```
lblLength.textProperty().bind(
        Bindings.concat("Count: ", textField.textProperty().length()));
```

In our first width example, we can use the `format()` output method, reusing syntax from the Java, `java.util.Formatter`:

```
Bindings.format("Window size is %1$.0fx%2$.0f", stage.widthProperty(),
    stage.heightProperty());
```

The preceding code produces the following window, which is automatically updated on resizing:

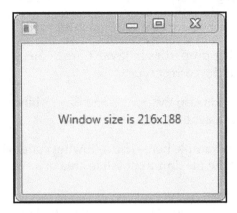

Window size is 216x188

Arithmetic operations

JavaFX binding supports basic arithmetic operations such as add, subtract, divide, multiply, and negate.

You can find them in binding/expression classes related to `Number`:

```
DoubleExpression, FloatExpression, IntegerExpression, LongExpression
```

The base class is `NumberExpression`. There are several overloaded methods to support work with both `Observable` objects and constants.

The very basic add operation is defined in `NumberExpression` and takes `NumberExpression` as a parameter. Here comes a question of the exact type of the result such an operation will produce. The rule is the same as in Java—*data type with most precision and capacity takes precedence:*

```
Double > Float > Long > Integer
```

Both operands are checked according to this chain and, if any of them hits, it means the result will be of that type.

For example, the following operation will produce `DoubleBinding`:

```
IntegerProperty intProp = new SimpleIntegerProperty(5);
DoubleProperty doubleProp = new SimpleDoubleProperty(1.5);
NumberBinding addBinding = intProp.add(doubleProp); // DoubleBinding
```

Fortunately, almost all number properties in JavaFX are `DoubleProperty`, so you don't need to care that much about the correct type.

The `Bindings` utility class adds also the `min()` and `max()` binding methods, which work both for properties and for constants.

Let's look at a more complex example here. The following code will create a 7x7 grid of rectangles that will try to fill the maximum possible area of a stage during resizing. We need three bindings for that:

- One to calculate which side of the window is smaller now
- One, applied to all rectangles, to change the rectangles' sizes accordingly
- One, again applied to all rectangles, to choose the rectangles' positions correctly:

```
// chapter3/operations/Rectangles.java
public void start(Stage stage) {
    Pane root = new Pane();

    final int count = 7; //number of rectangles

    // this is binding to calculate rectangle size
    // based on their count and minimal of scene width and height
    NumberBinding minSide = Bindings
            .min(root.heightProperty(), root.widthProperty())
            .divide(count);
    for (int x = 0; x < count; x++) {
        for (int y = 0; y < count; y++) {
            Rectangle rectangle = new Rectangle(0, 0, Color.LIGHTGRAY);

            // binding rectangle location to it's side size
            rectangle.xProperty().bind(minSide.multiply(x));
            rectangle.yProperty().bind(minSide.multiply(y));

            // binding rectangle's width and height
            rectangle.heightProperty().bind(minSide.subtract(2));
            rectangle.widthProperty().bind(rectangle.heightProperty());

            root.getChildren().add(rectangle);
        }
    }
```

```
        stage.setScene(new Scene(root, 500, 500));
        stage.show();
    }
```

Here are a few examples of this application's window in different sizes:

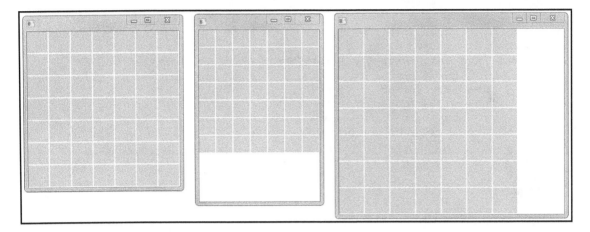

Try to run this application and check the logic behind it to get a better grasp on bindings.

Boolean operations

Boolean operations allow you to incorporate conditions directly into the binding.

First of all, there are `BooleanExpression/BooleanBinding` classes to represent observable boolean values. Then, to make if-then-else condition handlers, there are special methods in the Binding API:

```
when( CONDITION ) -> then( A ) -> otherwise( B )
```

Here, `when`, `then`, and `otherwise` are actual method names, not pseudocode. This construction means the following:

- Listen to A and B
- If A is changed and the CONDITION is true, update the bound value with A
- If B is changed and the CONDITION is false, update the bound value with B

As an example, let's forget for a minute we have the `min()` method from the rectangles grid example and re-implement it using boolean operations:

```
// original code
NumberBinding min = Bindings.min(root.heightProperty(),
root.widthProperty());

// boolean bindings version
NumberBinding minSide = Bindings
    .when( root.heightProperty().lessThan(root.widthProperty()) ) //
CONDITION
        .then( root.heightProperty() )       // option A
        .otherwise( root.widthProperty() ); // option B
```

Note the `lessThan()` call in the condition. It's one of the great range-of-conditional Boolean operations provided by JavaFX. Here is a self-explanatory list of them:

```
equal()
notEqual()
equalIgnoreCase()
notEqualIgnoreCase()

greaterThan()
greaterThanOrEqual()
lessThan()
lessThanOrEqual()

isEmpty()
isNotEmpty()
isNull()
isNotNull()

not()
or()
and()
```

I consciously dropped parameter types here as there is a huge list of overloaded methods for each possible type, for your convenience. All these methods are accessible from the `Bindings` class and the most common ones from `Expression` classes of corresponding types.

Working with bidirectional binding and converters

Bidirectional binding is very convenient for properties of the same type, but you are not restricted by that. You can bind bidirectionally properties of String and any other type by providing a corresponding converter.

There is a large list of predefined converters for the common types, for example, binding a number and a string:

```
Bindings.bindBidirectional(
        textProperty, numberProperty, new NumberStringConverter());
```

This converter also supports Locale and patterns from the java.text.DecimalFormat class. See the following application as an example:

```
// chapter3/other/BidiConverters.java
public void start(Stage stage) {
    Slider s1 = new Slider(0, 100, 40);
    TextField tf1 = new TextField();
    tf1.textProperty().bindBidirectional(s1.valueProperty(),
                            new NumberStringConverter());
    TextField tf2 = new TextField();
    tf2.textProperty().bindBidirectional(s1.valueProperty(),
                            new NumberStringConverter(Locale.US, "Value:
0000.#"));
    VBox root = new VBox(40, s1, tf1, tf2);
    root.setAlignment(Pos.CENTER);
    root.setPadding(new Insets(20));

    stage.setScene(new Scene(root, 200, 250));
    stage.show();
}
```

This code produces the following application, where you can edit any field or move the slider to update the same value shown in three different formats. Refer to the following screenshot:

Note that the converter will try to do its best to convert back and forth, but if you put the wrong value in the text field, nothing will be updated and `ParseException` will be thrown on the event thread (unfortunately, you can't catch or handle it there using the public API).

Also, you can provide your own converter by implementing the following very simple interface:

```java
// adding one more field to the previous example
TextField tf3 = new TextField();
tf3.textProperty().bindBidirectional(s1.valueProperty(), new
StringConverter<Number>() {
    @Override
    public String toString(Number number) {
        return number + " is good number";
    }

    @Override
    public Number fromString(String string) {
        return Double.valueOf(string.split(" ")[0]);
    }
});
```

This code adds one more `TextField` to our previous example, which is governed by our new custom converter:

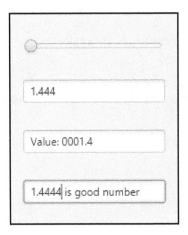

Creating custom bindings

If you have a complex logic, you can create your own binding by either extending the corresponding abstract base class—`DoubleBinding`, `StringBinding`, `ObjectBinding`—there are several options for different types; or by using a utility method from the `Bindings` class.

Implementing base binding classes

The concept of binding is simple:

- Add a listener to change events you want to track
- Compute the value you want to have

Correspondingly, in the following example, we call `bind()` for the desired property and override `computeValue()` method:

```
public void start(Stage primaryStage) {
    Button btn = new Button();
    btn.setText("Click me");

    StackPane root = new StackPane();
    root.setBackground(Background.EMPTY);
```

```
    root.getChildren().add(btn);
    Scene scene = new Scene(root, 300, 250);

    ObjectBinding<Paint> objectBinding = new ObjectBinding<Paint>() {
        {
            bind(btn.pressedProperty());
        }
        @Override
        protected Paint computeValue() {
            return btn.isPressed() ? Color.RED : Color.GREEN;
        }
    };
    scene.fillProperty().bind(objectBinding);

    primaryStage.setTitle("Hello World!");
    primaryStage.setScene(scene);
    primaryStage.show();
}
```

In this example, the scene background color changes if the button is pressed.

Bindings helper function

The `Bindings` class has a helper function for custom bindings:

```
// chapter3.other.CreateBinding.java
Bindings.createObjectBinding(
    ()-> btn.isPressed() ? Color.RED : Color.GREEN, // computeValue logic
    btn.pressedProperty()                           // list of observed
values
);
```

And, as a small reminder, let's rewrite this binding once again using the Boolean binding operations we reviewed in the preceding code:

```
scene.fillProperty().bind(
        Bindings.when(btn.pressedProperty())
            .then(Color.RED)
            .otherwise(Color.GREEN));
```

Understanding binding collections

JavaFX 10 supports three main collection types—List, Map, and Set.

You can make any Java collection observable using FXCollections helper methods:

```
List observableList = FXCollections.observableArrayList(collection);
```

This makes a collection trigger a listener on every addition, removal, or change in the elements order.

The FXCollections class mimics java.util.Collections a lot, providing observable counterparts for java.util.Collections methods.

Note you can go even deeper, observing not only a collection but the collection elements' changes as well, using the following method:

```
<E> ObservableList<E> observableList(List<E> list, Callback<E,
Observable[]> extractor)
```

Here, you need to additionally provide the extractor object, which will tells us which observable or observables in the element have to be tracked. Here is an example:

```
// chapter3/collections/Extractor.java
public void start(Stage stage) {
    // Lets have a list of Buttons
    List<Button> buttons = new ArrayList<>();
    for (int i = 0; i < 10; i++) {
        buttons.add(new Button(i + ""));
    }

    // Now lets have an observable collection which
    // will trigger listener when any button is pressed:
    ObservableList<Button> observableList =
FXCollections.observableList(buttons, (btn) -> {
        // in the extractor we need to return
        // a list of observables to be tracked
        return new Observable[] { btn.pressedProperty() };
    });

    // And add a listener
    IntegerProperty counter = new SimpleIntegerProperty(0);
    observableList.addListener((ListChangeListener.Change<? extends Button>
c) -> {
        counter.set(counter.intValue() + 1);
    });
```

```
Label label = new Label();
label.textProperty().bind(counter.asString("changes count: %1$s"));

HBox root = new HBox(10);
root.setAlignment(Pos.CENTER);
root.getChildren().add(label);
root.getChildren().addAll(buttons);
stage.setScene(new Scene(root, 500, 100));
stage.setTitle("Binding to a List demo");
stage.show();
}
```

This code will produce an application where one binding track clicks for any number of buttons:

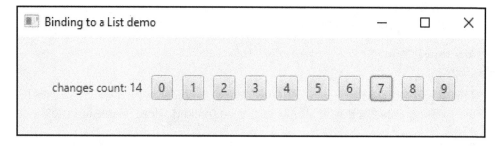

Once we have the observable list, we can use the binding as well. For example, in the following code, we connect two `ListView` objects to make them show similar data:

```
public void start(Stage stage) {
    ListView<String> listView = new ListView<>();
    listView.getItems().addAll("1", "2", "3");
    ListView<String> listView2 = new ListView<>();
    listView2.itemsProperty().bind(listView.itemsProperty());

    Button button = new Button("add");
    button.setOnAction((e)->listView.getItems().add("Item " +
listView.getItems().size()));

    BorderPane root = new BorderPane();
    root.setLeft(listView);
    root.setRight(listView2);
    root.setBottom(button);
    stage.setScene(new Scene(root, 500, 250));
    stage.show();
}
```

Try adding elements to one `ListView` in the resulting application and the changes will be reflected in the other one. Refer to the following screenshot:

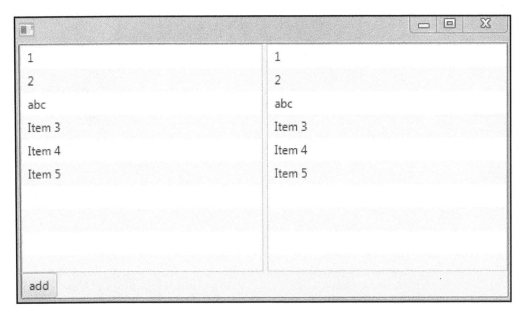

Summary

In this chapter, we looked at the binding functionality, which allows us to simplify the logic of the components' interactions. We learned that every property of JavaFX can be monitored for changes and quickly hooked to other properties through binding calls.

The Binding API is another step forward Java makes to the usability of the functional languages. The first was the Java8 Streams API. They both allow us to build a complex logic sequentially without using excessive syntax such as anonymous class creation.

In the following chapter, we will review another important tool introduced by JavaFX—the markup description language FXML.

4
FXML

FXML is a powerful tool used to build a complex JavaFX UI and separate business logic from UI design. This chapter will cover the following topics:

- Using FXML to design an FX application
- Working with SceneBuilder—the drag-and-drop designer provided by Oracle
- Viewing FXML as the **model-view-controller** (**MVC**) pattern

Introduction to FXML

When we were talking about Scenegraph, we saw how conveniently UI is represented by a tree graph structure. What else is good to describe tree structures? XML!

That is what FXML is all about. It allows us to describe the UI by the XML files. It's a common approach to describing static UI pages. For example, XAML for C#, or Android GUI, uses a similar approach.

Basics of FXML

In FXML, each XML node corresponds to a JavaFX entity:

- Adding a tag to the FXML file is similar to calling a constructor for a corresponding class.
- XML attributes correspond to the constructor parameters or setter method calls.
- For `Parent` classes, the inner nodes correspond to the children nodes, building hierarchy on the fly.
- For other classes, the inner nodes correspond to any entities these classes may contain. For example, you can populate `FXCollection` through FXML.

Let's compare an application and the FXML that describes it. Here is the application:

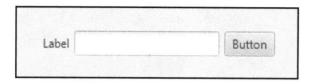

The FXML that describes it is as follows:

```
<?xml version="1.0" encoding="UTF-8"?>

<?import javafx.scene.control.*?>
<?import java.lang.*?>
<?import javafx.scene.layout.*?>

<HBox alignment="CENTER" spacing="5.0" onAction="#buttonHandler"
xmlns:fx="http://javafx.com/fxml" xmlns="http://javafx.com/javafx/8"
fx:controller="chapter4.first.FirstController">
    <children>
        <Label text="Label" />
        <TextField fx:id="textField" />
        <Button fx:id="button" text="Button" />
    </children>
</HBox>
```

Here, we have four nodes for JavaFX entities—HBox and its children, Label, TextField, and Button—and a service node, children, which corresponds to the children collection of the HBox.

To use this FXML in a program, you need to use FXMLLoader to get a top-level node as a result, which can be used just like a regular FXML node:

```
// chapter4/first/DemoFXML.java
HBox root = (HBox) FXMLLoader.load(
                    getClass().getResource("FirstDocument.fxml"));

Scene scene = new Scene(root, 300, 80);
stage.setScene(scene);
stage.show();
```

The next question is where to put the logic for FXML programs.

Note the `fx:controller` attribute of the FXML. It's the name of the special controller class that handles the business logic. The controller and FXML are connected through the tags, such as `fx:id`, which JavaFX uses to assign a JavaFX object to all FXML tags:

```java
// chapter4/first/FirstController.java
public class FirstController implements Initializable {
    @FXML
    private Button button;

    @FXML
    private TextField textField;
    @Override
    public void initialize(URL url, ResourceBundle rb) {
        button.setText("hello");
    }

    @FXML
    private void buttonHandler(ActionEvent event) {
        textField.setText("hello");
    }
}
```

Any field annotated by `@FXML` will automatically be initialized with a corresponding tag with the same `fx:id` as the field's name. At the time the `initialize` method is called, all these fields will be ready.

Note, at the moment of `initialize()` not all UI functionality is ready yet. For example, you can't set focus to a UI control. To address it, you can use the following trick—wrap such code with `Platform.runLater()` and it will be called on the next good opportunity. Note, though, it may not work for complex applications.

Also, methods with the same `@FXML` tags will be associated with the `#methodName` attribute's values in the FXML file. See the `buttonHandler` methods in the preceding examples.

Benefits of FXML

This division of the UI layout and the business logic pattern gives us several benefits.

First of all, separation of View and Controller logic gives more flexibility and supportability to your code. Once you have established an interface between View and Controller (which is defined by `fx-id` objects and handler names), you can modify them separately or share this work across the team.

Secondly, having an intermediate media to store app layout allows using separate tools to work with it. We will talk about SceneBuilder in detail later in this chapter, which allows designing JavaFX apps in WYSIWYG mode.

And finally, even without extra tools, FXML is much closer to actual application layout than Java code. You can clearly see which parent has which nodes, and all nodes' attributes are gathered in one place. In Java code, all this logic is often spread all over the method bodies or even between different classes.

Limitations of FXML

FXML can describe only static user interfaces; for any UI changes, you'll need to use Java code or prepare a separate FXML.

Also, debugging FXML loading is tricky as it works through reflection and you need to be very careful with the names of @FXML variables.

For the same reason, refactoring of the code that uses FXML may miss text constants inside FXML. Some IDEs (for example, the latest versions of NetBeans) may help with that.

Working with FXML loaders

There is only one class responsible for loading FXML—FXMLLoader—but working with it requires care, as shown in the following sections.

Working with resources

Let's look again at loading FXML:

```
FXMLLoader.load(getClass().getResource("FirstDocument.fxml")); // URL
```

The `load()` method's parameter here is a URL to the FXML file during **runtime**. It usually looks like the following:

```
jar:file:/path/to/jar/file/FxmlDemo.jar!/demo/FirstDocument.fxml
```

So, you will almost never set it directly as a `String` but through the `getResource()` method. The `getResource` parameter can be relative to the current class, as in the preceding examples, or absolute to your JAR directory structure, for example:

```
FXMLLoader.load(getClass().getResource("/demo/FirstDocument.fxml"));
```

Using absolute paths allows you to store FXML files in a separate folder rather than among the Java code, which is more convenient for complex projects.

Often, the project structure will look like the following:

```
./src/demo/FirstController.java
./src/demo/FxmlDemo.java
./resources/fxmls/FirstController.fxml
```

Here, the JAR routine will combine both built classes and FXML files into one folder, so the JAR content will look as follows:

```
FxmlDemo.jar!/demo/FirstController.java
FxmlDemo.jar!/demo/FxmlDemo.java
FxmlDemo.jar!/fxmls/FirstController.fxml
```

In this case, your FXML loader will have to address the FXML file by an absolute address:

```
FXMLLoader.load(getClass().getResource("/fxmls/FirstDocument.fxml"));
```

Using the FXMLLoader API

Aside from only loading and FXML, you may need to use other `FXMLLoader` functionality. In this case, you need to construct an object:

```
FXMLLoader loader = new
FXMLLoader(getClass().getResource("FXMLDocument.fxml"));
loader.load();
FirstController controller = loader.getController();
Parent root = loader.getRoot();
```

Due to an unfortunate name choice, there are several overridden `load()` methods in FXML and most of them are static. Make sure you are using non-static methods for calls from the instantiated `FXMLLoader`. See the following example:

```
FXMLLoader loader = new FXMLLoader();
loader.load(getClass().getResource("FXMLDocument.fxml"));
// STATIC method!
FirstController controller = loader.getController(); //
returns null
Parent root = loader.getRoot(); // returns null
```

Working with the fx:root attribute and custom components

You can revert the workflow of the FXML node creation and inject FXML content into your own object. This is especially useful if you want to create custom controls with content managed by FXML.

Firstly, the `fx:root` attribute should be used instead of the direct class name for the root node:

```
<?import javafx.scene.control.*?>
<?import javafx.scene.layout.*?>

<fx:root type="HBox" xmlns:fx="http://javafx.com/fxml">
    <children>
        <Label fx:id="label" />
        <TextField fx:id="textField" />
    </children>
</fx:root>
```

Also, note that you may not set `fx:controller` here and select the desired type of the root.

Now, we can create the class that will be used as a root for such FXML:

```
// chapter4/fxroot/MyControl.java
public class MyControl extends HBox {
    @FXML
    private TextField textField;

    @FXML
    private Label label;
```

```java
    public MyControl(String text) throws IOException {
        // here we initialize our HBox
        setAlignment(Pos.CENTER);
        setSpacing(5);
        // loading FXML and using current object as it's root and
controller
        FXMLLoader fxmlLoader = new
FXMLLoader(getClass().getResource("MyControl.fxml"));
        fxmlLoader.setRoot(this);
        fxmlLoader.setController(this);
        fxmlLoader.load();
        // now we already can use @FXML initialized controls
        textField.setText(text);
        label.setText("Message: ");
    }
}
```

Here, we are using the same class for the Controller and Root, which allows us to contain all logic in one place. So, we can create our new control like a regular JavaFX class:

```java
// chapter4/fxroot/FxRootDemo.java
public class FxRootDemo extends Application {
    @Override
    public void start(Stage stage) throws Exception {
        StackPane stackPane = new StackPane();
        stackPane.getChildren().add(
                new MyControl("Hello, World"));
        Scene scene = new Scene(stackPane, 300, 80);
        stage.setScene(scene);
        stage.show();
    }
}
```

And, we will get the following application:

Note that your own controls can be used in FXML as well. You just need to provide the correct includes.

Working with Controllers

A question that is often asked is how to transfer data between an FXML Controller and other parts of the application. Let's look into the available options.

Enhancing Controllers

FXML Controllers are not set in stone; you can add methods to them and use them to transfer information.

Consider the following example for the `FirstDocument.fxml` we used earlier in this chapter:

```
public class SmartController implements Initializable {
    public void setText(String newText) {
        textField.setText(newText);
    }

    @FXML
    private Button button;

    @FXML
    private TextField textField;
    @Override
    public void initialize(URL url, ResourceBundle rb) {
        button.setText("hello");
    }
}
```

Now, we can work with the FXML variables from other classes, as in the following example, from `Application`:

```
FXMLLoader loader = new
FXMLLoader(getClass().getResource("FirstDocument.fxml"));
HBox root = loader.load();
loader.<SmartController>getController().setText("Text from App");
```

Also, you can always declare variables in a `Controller` public and use them directly. While it's not advised for production code, it can simplify prototyping.

Using a preconstructed Controller

The approach from the previous section will not work if you need to have certain data accessible at the time of the `initialize()` call. If the controller is set by the `fx:controller` attribute in FXML, it will be constructed automatically by JavaFX.

For such cases, there is an option to use a preconstructed controller:

```java
public class PreconstructedController implements Initializable {
    private final String newText;
    public PreconstructedController(String newText) {
        this.newText = newText;
    }

    @FXML
    private Button button;

    @FXML
    private TextField textField;
    @Override
    public void initialize(URL url, ResourceBundle rb) {
        button.setText(newText);
    }
}
```

Also, you need to remove the `fx:controller` attribute from the FXML file.

After that, you can create and initialize your controller in advance and then use it for FXML:

```java
FXMLLoader loader = new
FXMLLoader(getClass().getResource("FirstDocument.fxml"));
PreconstructedController pc = new PreconstructedController("new text");
loader.setController(pc);
HBox root = loader.load();
```

Working with data

An FXML node resembles the MVC pattern very closely. FXML as a View and the Controller present by default, the only thing left is Model—a separate entity to store data and communicate with the outside part of an application.

It can be either a global context in a form of a `Singleton` class or a combination with one of the previous methods to set your model class to a controller.

Syntax details of FXML

All the FXML syntax we have already used in this chapter was very self-explanatory (another benefit of FXML!) but, there are additional useful options which we will review in the following sections.

Reviewing the basics of FXML

Let's briefly review the basics we learned at the beginning of this chapter:

- Tags correspond to JavaFX classes and attributes correspond to these classes' properties
- By setting the `fx:id` attribute, you can link a field from the Controller to these tags
- You can set the Controller by the `fx:controller` attribute of the root node
- Action handlers can be linked using the # symbol

Take a look at the following code snippet:

```
<HBox alignment="CENTER" spacing="5.0" onAction="#buttonHandler"
          xmlns:fx="http://javafx.com/fxml"
xmlns="http://javafx.com/javafx/8"
          fx:controller="chapter4.first.FirstController">
   <children>
      <Label text="Label" />
      <TextField fx:id="textField" />
      <Button fx:id="button" text="Button" />
   </children>
</HBox>
```

Also, note the root tag should have XML namespace attributes set: xmlns:fx and xmlns.

Importing packages

The next thing you need to pay attention to is the imports section. All used classes should have corresponding packages mentioned in the import header:

```
<?import javafx.scene.control.*?>
<?import javafx.scene.layout.*?>
```

Including other FXML files

You can include one FXML in another, as shown in the following code:

```
<?import javafx.scene.layout.*?>
<HBox xmlns:fx="http://javafx.com/fxml">
    <children>
        <fx:include source="my_fields.fxml"/>
        <TextField fx:id="textField" />
        <Button fx:id="button" text="Button" />
    </children>
</HBox>
```

Here, my_fields.xml contains all the listed data:

```
<?import javafx.scene.control.*?>
<Label text="Label" />
```

Note that in this document, Label is a root element for simplicity. But, if you want to have several controls, you'll have to introduce a layout manager to handle them—there can be only one root element in the FXML.

But, what to do if the included FXML has its own Controller? They are called nested controllers and can be handled through the fx:id attribute, similar to regular JavaFX classes.

First of all, you need to set a name for your `include`:

```
<?import javafx.scene.layout.*?>
<?import javafx.scene.control.*?>
<HBox xmlns:fx="http://javafx.com/fxml"
fx:controller="chapter4.includes.FirstController">
    <children>
        <fx:include fx:id="myLabel" source="MyLabel.fxml"/>
        <TextField fx:id="textField" />
        <Button text="Button" onAction="#btnAction"/>
    </children>
</HBox>
```

Now, let's create a slightly more sophisticated `MyLabel` FXML with a `Controller`:

```
<?import javafx.scene.layout.*?>
<?import javafx.scene.control.*?>
<VBox xmlns:fx="http://javafx.com/fxml"
fx:controller="chapter4.includes.NestedController">
    <Label text="MyLabel" />
    <Button fx:id="myBtn" text="I'm nested" onAction="#myBtnAction" />
</VBox>
```

And, `NestedController` provides a small API to alter its button:

```
// chapter4/includes/NestedController.java
public class NestedController implements Initializable {
    @FXML
    private Button myBtn;
    @FXML
    void myBtnAction(ActionEvent event) {
        System.out.println("Hello from " + myBtn.getText());
    }
    public void setButtonText(String text) {
        myBtn.setText(text);
    }

    @Override
    public void initialize(URL url, ResourceBundle rb) {
    }
}
```

Now, in the controller for the first FXML, we can use that API:

```java
// chapter4/includes/FirstController.java
public class FirstController implements Initializable {
    @FXML
    private NestedController myLabelController; // name is tricky! See below.
    @FXML
    void btnAction(ActionEvent event) {
        myLabelController.setButtonText(textField.getText());
    }
    @FXML
    private TextField textField;
    @Override
    public void initialize(URL url, ResourceBundle rb) {
    }
}
```

Note that the name of the corresponding variable should be the corresponding fx:id value concatenated with the *Controller* word.

Using FXML defines

To structure your FXML better, you can use fx:define to separate usage and declaration of various elements. For example, the preceding examples with includes can be rewritten by defining the include first and using it later through the $ prefix. Refer to the following code snippet:

```xml
<?import javafx.scene.layout.*?>
<?import javafx.scene.control.*?>
<HBox xmlns:fx="http://javafx.com/fxml"
fx:controller="chapter4.includes.FirstController">
    <fx:define>
        <fx:include fx:id="myLabel" source="MyLabel.fxml"/>
    </fx:define>
    <children>
        <StackPane children="$myLabel">
    </children>
</HBox>
```

Another common use case for `define` is setting a toggle group for radio buttons:

```
<?import javafx.scene.layout.*?>
<?import javafx.scene.control.*?>
<HBox xmlns:fx="http://javafx.com/fxml" >
    <fx:define>
        <ToggleGroup fx:id="toggleGroup"/>
    </fx:define>
    <children>
        <RadioButton text="radio1" toggleGroup="$toggleGroup"/>
        <RadioButton text="radio2" toggleGroup="$toggleGroup"/>
        <RadioButton text="radio3" toggleGroup="$toggleGroup"/>
    </children>
</HBox>
```

Default properties

In some cases, you can skip declaring properties, such as `children`:

```
<?import javafx.scene.layout.*?>
<?import javafx.scene.control.*?>
<HBox xmlns:fx="http://javafx.com/fxml"
fx:controller="chapter4.includes.FirstController">
    <TextField fx:id="textField" />
    <Button text="Button" onAction="#btnAction"/>
</HBox>
```

The most common properties are marked as *default* by the JavaFX API, and FXML allows us to skip them to remove obvious parts of the code.

You can detect such properties by looking into JavaDoc or the source code. They are set through the `@javafx.beans.DefaultProperty` annotation:

```
@DefaultProperty("children")
public class Pane
extends Region
```

Using this annotation, you can set the default property for your own classes as well.

Referring to resources from FXML

Certain JavaFX controls work with external resources. For example, the `Image` class requires a URL of the represented image. To simplify work with such controls in FXML, you can refer to a path relative to the FXML location by using the @ prefix. Refer to the following code snippet:

```
<ImageView>
    <Image url="@image.png"/>
</ImageView>
```

Here, JavaFX assumes that `image.png` is located in the same folder (either on disk or in a JAR) as the FXML.

Adding business logic to FXML

Although I strongly advise against doing it, you can put bits of the business logic directly into FXML by using the JavaScript engine and the `fx:script` tag.

In the next example, we declare a handler directly in the FXML and assign it to the button:

```
<?language javascript?>
<?import javafx.scene.control.*?>
<?import javafx.scene.layout.*?>

<HBox alignment="CENTER" spacing="5.0" xmlns:fx="http://javafx.com/fxml/1">
    <fx:script>
        function handleButtonAction(event) {
            textField.setText("clicked");
        }
    </fx:script>
    <children>
        <Label text="Label" />
        <TextField fx:id="textField" />
        <Button fx:id="button" text="Button"
                onAction="handleButtonAction(event);"/>
    </children>
</HBox>
```

And, on button click, the `TextField` value will be updated:

Also, you can use binding by using expression bindings:

```
<?import javafx.scene.control.*?>
<?import javafx.scene.layout.*?>

<HBox alignment="CENTER" spacing="5.0" xmlns:fx="http://javafx.com/fxml/1">
    <children>
        <Label text="${textField.text}" />
        <TextField fx:id="textField" />
    </children>
</HBox>
```

Here, we bind the `Label` text property to the TextField content.

There are also ways to build a more complex business logic inside FXML, but I really advise not using these options for the following reasons:

- You can't debug this logic
- It's not tracked by the IDE's Find Usage or Refactor mechanisms
- It's easy to miss them in a text file
- It can be very confusing to maintain

Using static methods in FXML

Some JavaFX APIs require the use of static methods, like those we used to adjust BorderPane in Chapter 1, *Stages, Scenes, and Layout*:

```
BorderPane.setAlignment(label, Pos.CENTER);
```

To use them in FXML, you need to call them backward—inside a parameter to be adjusted, you need to assign a value to the class name and property name combination—`BorderPane.alignment="CENTER"`.

Here is a full example of such FXML (note another example of using `define`, adding it to make an image look better):

```
<?import javafx.scene.control.*?>
<?import javafx.scene.layout.*?>
<?import javafx.geometry.*?>

<BorderPane padding="$insets" xmlns:fx="http://javafx.com/fxml/1">
    <fx:define>
        <Insets bottom="5.0" left="5.0" right="5.0" top="5.0"
fx:id="insets"/>
    </fx:define>
    <top>
        <Label text="Label" BorderPane.alignment="CENTER"/>
    </top>
    <bottom>
        <TextField fx:id="textField" />
    </bottom>
</BorderPane>
```

On running the preceding code, you'll see the following output:

SceneBuilder

Finally, having gone through most of the features of FXML, we will look into a great tool to handle them—SceneBuilder. It's an open source tool, primarily developed by Oracle. It can be downloaded from the Oracle site or built from sources—see the instructions at `https://wiki.openjdk.java.net/display/OpenJFX/Building+OpenJFX`.

Working with a WYSIWYG editor

The **What You See Is What You Get** (**WYSIWYG**) conception is extremely useful for building UIs. You can design your application by dragging and dropping components and adjusting their properties:

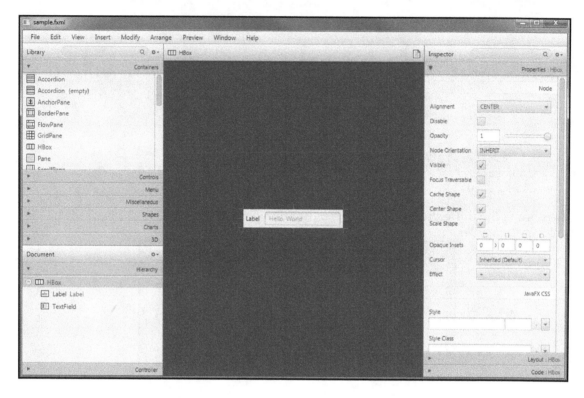

This is a base SceneBuilder UI. It contains the following components:

- Drawing board in the middle
- List of available components in the top-left corner
- List of properties for the currently selected component in the right-hand side panel
- Scenegraph representation, called Hierarchy (it works in a similar way to the ScenicView tool we used in previous chapters), in the bottom-left corner

The main functionality is pretty straightforward, so I'll review only the less-noticeable features.

Features

You can preview the current state of the FXML app by using the **Preview** menu item:

The **Components** window has a convenient search box at the top to avoid looking through the categories:

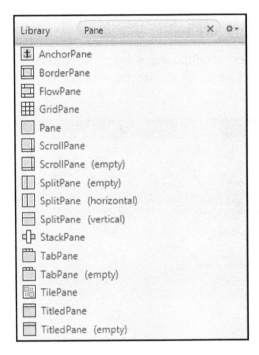

Below **Hierarchy,** there is a **Controller** view.

It allows you to set the `Controller` name—be careful of typos; it's just a text field for `SceneBuilder`. Also, all fields that you intend to use in the `Controller` and marked with `fx:id` will be listed here:

Based on this information, SceneBuilder can prepare for you a skeleton of a real `Controller` based on your FXML. Use the menu item **View | Show Sample Controller Skeleton**:

Make sure you are satisfied with your FXML state first—if you used this generated `Controller` class, added code to it, and changed the FXML after, there is no automated way to merge your changes with the updated generated `Controller`.

Specifying CSS files through the Preview menu

You can specify CSS files and localization files directly in SceneBuilder through the **Preview** menu. Note that these changes will not be reflected in the FXML you are editing as they have to be set in the Java code—they are added only for convenience.

We will talk in detail about CSS in Chapter 6, *Styling Applications with CSS*, for this section, you need to know just a few facts:

- JavaFX supports CSS similar to HTML
- You can assign various properties to CSS classes and assign these classes to JavaFX objects

Here is a sample CSS used for the following screenshot:

```
.custom-field {
    -fx-font: 16px "Courier New";
}
```

Once you've selected a CSS file, it will instantly be applied to your editing interface. Also, all CSS classes will be available on the **Property** page, so you can select them from the list instead of typing—no typos! Check the bottom of the popup in the following screenshot:

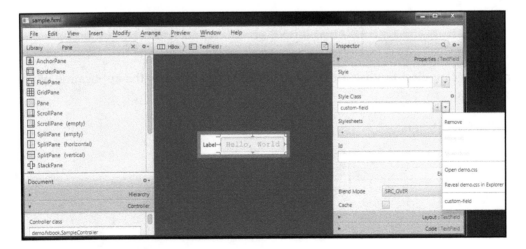

In this screenshot, `custom-field` is a class from the CSS file that alters the `TextField` font.

Localization in Preview

For localization, you can change any text fields to i18n labels by using the small gear icon:

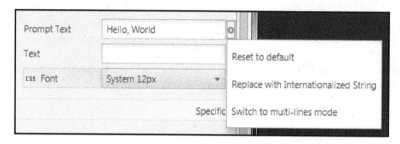

For example, let's look at the following two i18n files:

```
#demo_en.properties
label.text=LABEL
tf1.text=HELLO

#demo_fr.properties
label.text=étiqueter
tf1.text=bonjour
```

Let's apply them to our small UI. First, we change all text values to i18n variables:

And now, we can select English and French versions and preview the application without even compiling any code!

Here is the English version:

Here is the French version:

This way, you can be sure that your UI looks good in all supported localizations.

In Java code, you can set the resource bundle used for a specific FXML localization in the Loader API:

```
// for current system locale
loader.setResources(ResourceBundle.getBundle("chapter4.demo"));
// for specific locale
loader.setResources(ResourceBundle.getBundle("chapter4.demo", new
Locale("fr", "FR")));
```

Here, `chapter4` is a package name and `demo` is the first part of the filename (`demo_fr.properties`).

Summary

In this chapter, we studied FXML syntax and capabilities, studied common questions, and learned about the SceneBuilder tool. With these tools, building a UI with FXML became easier due to using a WYSIWYG editor and decoupling the UI from the code.

In the next chapter, we'll look into the Animation API, which helps with dynamic content.

5
Animation

Modern applications often introduce dynamic elements to boost usability or just to make things look better. Ranging from *slide to unlock* to dynamic charts, updating the animation has become an integral part of a good interface.

In this chapter, we will review what APIs JavaFX provides for animation, covering the following topics:

- What an animation is in JavaFX terms
- Building timelines
- Using interpolators
- Working with transitions—simplified timelines

What is an animation?

From a JavaFX point of view, an animation is a change of a property over a period of time; for example:

- If you want an object to move, you need to work with coordinate properties.
- If you want to shrink or enlarge an object, you can use the scale property.
- You can even use the Animation API for objects which don't have a visual representation at all.

You need the following three API classes to create an animation:

- `KeyFrame` represents a point in time
- `KeyValue` describes the value the desired property should have at the moment described by `KeyFrame`

- `Timeline` collects all `KeyFrame` objects and runs the animation, calculating all intermediate values for properties between `KeyFrame` objects.

In the next section, we will review these concepts with an example.

Animation example

Let's look at the following code and corresponding comments:

```java
// chapter5/basics/BasicAnimation.java
public void start(Stage stage) {
    Circle circle = new Circle(50, 150, 50, Color.RED);

    // change circle.translateXProperty from it's current value to 200
    KeyValue keyValue = new KeyValue(circle.translateXProperty(), 200);

    // over the course of 5 seconds
    KeyFrame keyFrame = new KeyFrame(Duration.seconds(5), keyValue);
    Timeline timeline = new Timeline(keyFrame);

    Scene scene = new Scene(new Pane(circle), 300, 250);
    stage.setScene(scene);
    stage.show();

    timeline.play();
}
```

It's not very convenient to show how animation works using screenshots, so I really encourage you to run the code from the preceding sample and see it in motion. Refer to the following screenshot:

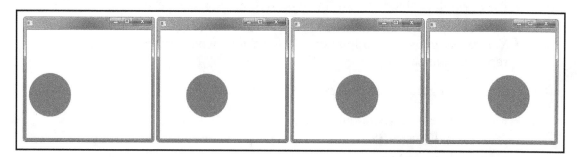

In the next section, we will review the API used in this example in more detail.

Understanding KeyFrame and KeyValue

KeyFrame works tightly with the Duration class, which is responsible for measuring time intervals. The Duration API is straightforward—you choose a time unit, how many of them you need, and how to combine them. See the following examples:

```
Duration.seconds(5);
Duration.hours(1).add(Duration.minutes(15));
Duration.valueOf("10ms");
new Duration(100); // default unit is milliseconds
Duration.ZERO;
```

For a specified Duration, you can select one or several KeyValue objects. KeyValue takes two parameters—the property you want to set and a value of the corresponding type.

Note that you don't have to set initial values in the first KeyFrame with Duration.ZERO—if they are missing, Timeframe will use the current values of these properties. For example, for the sample from the previous section, this autogenerated KeyFrame may look as follows:

```
new KeyFrame(Duration.ZERO, new KeyValue(circle.translateXProperty(),
circle.getTranslateX()));
```

Also, you don't have to use the same properties for each KeyFrame, but Timeline will calculate each used property for *each* KeyFrame. For example, look at the following code:

```
// chapter5/basics/CombinedAnimation.java
KeyFrame keyFrame = new KeyFrame(Duration.seconds(5),
    new KeyValue(circle.translateXProperty(), 200));

KeyFrame keyFrame2 = new KeyFrame(Duration.seconds(10),
    new KeyValue(circle.translateYProperty(), 200));

Timeline timeline = new Timeline(keyFrame, keyFrame2);
```

The first impression is that the circle will move horizontally for the first 5 seconds, then vertically for another 5. But instead, `Timeline` will move the circle horizontally for 5 seconds and simultaneously move it vertically for 10 seconds. The final trajectory of the circle will be as follows (shown in gray):

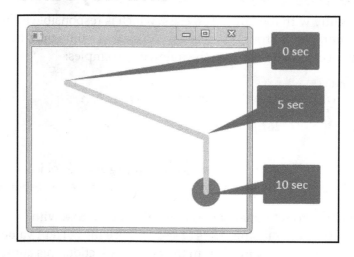

Here, you can see that the horizontal coordinate changed for 5 seconds only, but the vertical coordinate changed from 0 to 10 seconds.

Adding handlers and timers

In addition to `KeyValue`, `KeyFrame` allows us to set a handler which will trigger at the selected `Duration`. For example, in the preceding timeline, we can change the object color in the middle:

```
KeyFrame keyFrame = new KeyFrame(Duration.seconds(5),
        (ActionEvent event) -> {
            circle.setFill(Color.GREEN);
        },
        new KeyValue(circle.translateXProperty(), 200));
KeyFrame keyFrame2 = new KeyFrame(Duration.seconds(10),
            new KeyValue(circle.translateYProperty(), 200));
Timeline timeline = new Timeline(keyFrame, keyFrame2);
```

This allows us to make simple timers for events on a UI thread:

```
Timeline timer = new Timeline(new KeyFrame(Duration.seconds(1),
    (event) -> {
        System.out.println("every second on the UI thread");
})); // no keyvalues is ok

timer.setCycleCount(Timeline.INDEFINITE);
timer.play();
```

Working with the Timeline API

Once `Timeline` is set up, you can control its flow using the following methods:

```
timeline.play();
timeline.pause();
timeline.stop();
```

Note that `stop()` resets `Timeline`, while `pause()` allows `Timeline` to be played again from the same point by another `play()` call.

Two other important properties are the following:

- `autoReverse:`Allows an animated object to go back and forth smoothly
- `cycleCount`: Repetition count. The default value is 1 and the maximalvalue is infinite; it can be set through the `Timeline.INDEFINITE` constant:

    ```
    timeline.setCycleCount(Timeline.INDEFINITE);
    timeline.setAutoReverse(true);
    ```

To check whether `Timeline` is playing, you can use the `Timeline.getStatus()` method, which returns one of the following three values:

```
Animation.Status.RUNNING // after play()
Animation.Status.PAUSED  // after pause()
Animation.Status.STOPPED // initial Timeline state and one after stop()
```

For example, to start and pause `Timeline` on mouse clicks, you can use the following code:

```
// Also note that is how mouse events are handled in JavaFX:
// you choose an object and provide a corresponding MouseEvent handler
root.setOnMouseClicked((event) -> {
        if (timeline.getStatus() == Animation.Status.RUNNING)
            timeline.pause();
        else
            timeline.play();});
```

Adding cue points

For finer control, you can use cue points for a specific duration:

```
timeline.playFrom(duration);
timeline.jumpTo(duration);

timeline.playFrom(cuePoint);
timeline.playFromStart();
```

Here, the cue point is a string; it can be set as a `KeyFrame` additional parameter:

```
KeyFrame keyFrame = new KeyFrame(Duration.seconds(5), "cue point 1",
keyValue);
...
timeline.playFrom("cue point 1");
```

Although cue points are being created in the `KeyFrame` objects, you can work with them only from the corresponding `Timeline`, for example, to print all cue points:

```
// chapter5/basics/CombinedAnimation.java
for (Map.Entry<String, Duration> entry :
timeline.getCuePoints().entrySet()) {
    System.out.println(entry.getValue() + ": " + entry.getKey());
}
```

Using the Interpolator API

By default, `Timeline` calculates how property values change between `KeyFrame` objects using a linear function—changing property values proportionally to the time passed.

You can control that more precisely using the Interpolator API.

Predefined interpolators

You can set interpolators when creating `KeyValue`:

```
new KeyValue(node.translateYProperty(), 200, Interpolator.LINEAR);
```

The default interpolator is `Interpolator.LINEAR`.

Visually, it looks like an abrupt stop at the end of the animation. To soften that, you can use one of the *easing* interpolators:

- `Interpolator.EASE_IN`: Starts slowly
- `Interpolator.EASE_OUT`: Ends slowly
- `Interpolator.EASE_BOTH`: Starts and ends slowly

You can see them all at work simultaneously by running the following code:

```java
// chapter5/basics/InterpolatorsDemo.java
public void start(Stage primaryStage) {
    VBox root = new VBox(10);
    Timeline timeline = new Timeline();
    timeline.setCycleCount(Timeline.INDEFINITE);
    timeline.setAutoReverse(true);

    Stream.of(
        Interpolator.LINEAR,
        Interpolator.EASE_IN,
        Interpolator.EASE_BOTH,
        Interpolator.EASE_OUT
    ).forEach((interpolator) -> {
        Circle node = new Circle(30, Color.RED);
        root.getChildren().add(node);
        KeyFrame keyFrame = new KeyFrame(Duration.seconds(2),
                new KeyValue(node.translateXProperty(), 240,
    interpolator)));
        timeline.getKeyFrames().add(keyFrame);
    });
    primaryStage.setScene(new Scene(root, 400, 400));
    primaryStage.show();
    timeline.play();
}
```

Note that we start the animation after `stage.show()`. It's a good way to make sure everything is ready and initialized so your animation will not be botched by other operations on the UI thread.

Here are several screenshots of this app running:

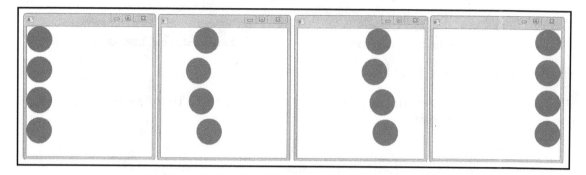

Note that all circles touch the right wall simultaneously—interpolators are responsible only for the calculation of the intermediate states of the properties; starting and ending values are set by `KeyValue` objects.

The last predefined interpolator is `Interpolator.DISCRETE`. It's very simple and doesn't calculate anything in between—it just instantly changes the value of the property once `Duration` has passed.

Using transitions – the predefined animations

Transitions are helper classes to simplify the most common animations:

- Movement
- Size change
- Rotation
- Color change

Using movement and resize transitions

Moving objects is a definition of an animation. So it's only logical to start from movement transitions:

- `TranslateTransition`: Plain move
- `PathTransition`: Moving along the path

- `RotateTransition`: Rotating objects
- `ScaleTransition`: Changing objects' size

Using TranslateTransition

The most straightforward transition is `TranslateTransition`. You choose what and where to move using the `translateX` and `translateY` properties and call `play()`. For example, if we look at the `Timeline` from the start of this chapter:

```
KeyValue keyValue = new KeyValue(node.translateXProperty(), 200);
KeyFrame keyFrame = new KeyFrame(Duration.seconds(5), keyValue);
Timeline timeline = new Timeline(keyFrame);
```

Using `TranslateTransition`, it will look as follows (you can compare similar parameters marked by the bold text):

```
// chapter5/transitions/TranslateTransitionDemo.java
TranslateTransition transition = new
TranslateTransition(Duration.seconds(5), node);
transition.setToX(200);
transition.play();
```

The Transition API is slightly more convenient and also has several helper methods as shown in the following code:

```
// instead of the end point you can set desired delta
transition.setByX(200);

// you can set both start and end point
// and, of course, set X and Y coordinates for the same transition
transition.setFromY(50);
transition.setToY(200);
```

Using PathTransition

The `PathTransition` transition allows you to set any trajectory for your node to follow during a transition:

```
// chapter5/transitions/PathTransitionDemo.java
SVGPath svgPath = new SVGPath();
svgPath.setFill(Color.LIGHTGRAY);
// You can recall this path from Chapter 2
svgPath.setContent("M30,30 H80 A280,120 0 0,1 80,130 V180 H30 Z");
```

```
Node node = new Circle(10, Color.BLACK);
PathTransition pt = new PathTransition(Duration.seconds(4), svgPath, node);
```

Here are several screenshots of this transition in action:

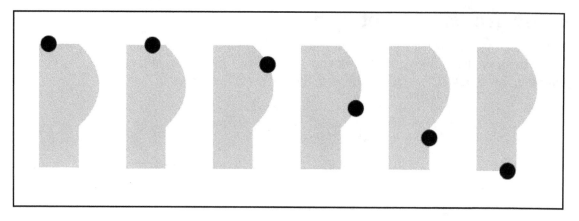

Note that any `Shape` can be used as a path for `PathTransition`, not just `Path` or `SVGPath`, for example:

```
PathTransition pt = new PathTransition(Duration.seconds(4), new Circle(50),
node);
```

Using RotateTransition

The next transition from this group is `RotateTransition`. It just rotates things:

```
// chapter5/transitions/RotateTransitionDemo.java
Node node = new Rectangle(50,50,120,80);
RotateTransition rt = new RotateTransition(Duration.seconds(3), node);
rt.setByAngle(180);
rt.play();
```

The only unconventional method here is an option to set an axis using a 3D point, so JavaFX will automatically show a projection of the virtual 3D rotation:

```
rt.setAxis(new Point3D(70, 80, 100));
```

While using the JavaFX API, you can often see a Z dimension in addition to X and Y. You can't really use Z unless you have a 3D scene set up (we will briefly review 3D in `Chapter 12`, *3D at a Glance*). The rotation axis is one exception.

Using ScaleTransition

The scale can be changed by the vertical and horizontal dimension separately as shown in the following code snippet:

```
ScaleTransition st = new ScaleTransition(Duration.seconds(3), node);
st.setToX(2); // double the size of the node
st.play();
```

While using the byX/byY methods, keep in mind that you are starting from a scale equal to 1 in both dimensions, for example:

```
st.setByX(1); // double the size of the node
st.setByX(-1); // change size to 0
```

Working with color transitions

The following transitions fall into this category: FadeTransition, FillTransition, and StrokeTransition.

The FillTransition transition makes a smooth change between two colors:

```
// chapter5/transitions/ColorTransitionsDemo.java
Shape circle = new Circle(50, 150, 50);
FillTransition ft = new FillTransition(Duration.seconds(3), circle,
Color.RED, Color.BLUE);
ft.play();
```

Intermediate values are calculated based on RGB and opacity numerical components of the Color through a special interpolator.

To make the Animation API aware of the interpolator support, the Color implements an Interpolatable interface, which you can use for your own components as well:

```
public interface Interpolatable<T> {
    public T interpolate(T endValue, double t);
}
```

The StrokeTransition transition works the same way as FillTransition but on the stroke of the Shape (the outer border; see Chapter 2, *Building Blocks – Shapes, Text, and Controls*).

The FadeTransition transition changes the opacity property of the Node.

Combining transitions

There are only two options here: `ParallelTransition`, which runs several animations in parallel, and `SequentialTransition`, which runs them one by one.

Note that these transitions work with the `Animation` class, which means you can combine both `Transition` and `Timeline`.

Both transitions take a node and a set of animations and apply these animations to that node unless some animation has a specific node already set for them.

There is a special transition which does nothing for a period of time: `PauseTransition`. Its only use is to conveniently add pauses to `SequentialTransition`.

Let's see it in a small example:

```
// chapter5/transitions/SequentialTransitionDemo
public void start(Stage primaryStage) {

    RotateTransition rotate = new RotateTransition(Duration.seconds(2));
    rotate.setByAngle(90);

    TranslateTransition translate = new
TranslateTransition(Duration.seconds(1));
    translate.setByX(100);

    ScaleTransition scale = new ScaleTransition(Duration.seconds(1));
    scale.setToX(0);
    scale.setToY(0);

    Node node = new Rectangle(50, 50, 100, 30);
    Scene scene = new Scene(new Pane(node), 300, 300);
    primaryStage.setScene(scene);
    primaryStage.show();

    SequentialTransition sequential = new SequentialTransition(
            translate, rotate, new PauseTransition(Duration.seconds(1)),
    scale);
    sequential.setNode(node);
    sequential.play();
}
```

Building an animated application

Let's combine several animations in a small application that shows how Earth rotates around the Sun (very roughly):

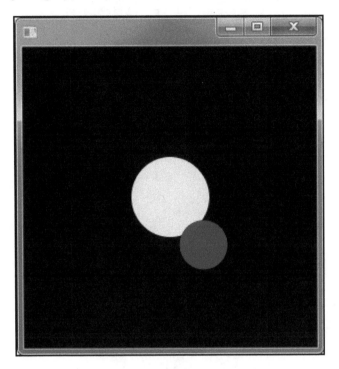

The first transition which we'll need is a `PathTransition` for Earth's orbit:

```
// chapter5/app/PlanetDemo.java
// preparing space, Sun and Earth
Pane root = new Pane();
Scene scene = new Scene(root, 300, 300, Color.BLACK);
Circle sun = new Circle(150,150, 40, Color.YELLOW);
Circle earth = new Circle(25, Color.BLUE);

// orbit and path transition
Ellipse orbit = new Ellipse(150, 150, 125, 50);
PathTransition pt = new PathTransition(Duration.seconds(5), orbit, earth);
pt.setInterpolator(Interpolator.LINEAR);
pt.setCycleCount(Timeline.INDEFINITE);
```

Now we have a planet orbiting the Sun. Let's scale it according to the perspective — bigger on the front part of the orbit and smaller on the back:

```
ScaleTransition st = new ScaleTransition(Duration.millis(2500),earth);
// we need to shift scaling because out path transition
// starts from the rightmost part of the ellipsis which
// the middle part of our scale transition
st.setDelay(Duration.millis(1250));
st.setToX(0.6);
st.setToY(0.6);
// scale is twice shorter than path because we are using autoReverse
st.setAutoReverse(true);
st.setCycleCount(Timeline.INDEFINITE);
```

Now we need to hide Earth behind the Sun during the second part of the path transition. Let's use a `Timeline` as a timer here:

```
Timeline front = new Timeline(
    new KeyFrame(Duration.millis(0), (e) -> earth.toFront()),
    new KeyFrame(Duration.millis(2500), (e) -> earth.toBack()),
    new KeyFrame(Duration.seconds(5))
);
front.setCycleCount(Timeline.INDEFINITE);
```

And the last step will be organizing all these animations into one to start them simultaneously:

```
ParallelTransition parallel = new ParallelTransition(pt, st, front);
parallel.playFrom(Duration.millis(1250));
```

Try to combine these code samples into a working program. Or you can find the full code sample on the book's GitHub page.

Summary

The Animation API provides a simple way to add dynamic elements to your application. It can be used in a wide range of applications, from games to interactive charts and controls. As we reviewed in this chapter, JavaFX provides a very convenient API to build animated applications. Basic animations can be achieved through transition classes and complex animations can be set up through timelines.

In the next chapter, we will review the CSS capabilities of JavaFX.

Styling Applications with CSS

6

CSS is a style sheet language that became a *de facto* standard in web development for describing the presentation aspect of a web page. It separates presentation and content, which greatly simplifies design and allows us to have a unified style through a whole page and site. CSS is mainly responsible for aspects such as fonts, color, heading styles, margins, padding, and other layout properties.

In this chapter, we will study how JavaFX technology innovatively used CSS to style not web but Java applications. We will cover the following topics:

- Introduction to CSS
- JavaFX specifics
- Using styles
- Advanced CSS syntax
- Benefits of using CSS
- Advanced JavaFX CSS API

At the end of the chapter, we will return to the Clock sample and learn how to style it with CSS.

Introduction to CSS

The main concept of the CSS markup language is matching UI elements to property values. Different ways to identify a UI element are called selectors and most CSS statements look as follows:

```
selector-name {
    property-name1: value1;
    property-name2: value2;
    /* ... */
}
```

To better see how it works, let's review a small example.

FirstStyles demonstration

In this demonstration, we will apply a CSS file to a JavaFX application, changing the styles of several buttons and a root node of the scene:

```
/* chapter6/basics/style.css */
.root {
    -fx-background-color: lightblue;
    -fx-padding: 10px;
}
.button {
    -fx-background-color: white
}
```

Note that all JavaFX CSS properties have the -fx prefix to be clearly distinguished from web CSS ones. JavaFX CSS and web CSS share syntax and property names and look very similar but JavaFX developers deliberately made styles and classes different in order to avoid any compatibility issues.

JavaFX CSS is described in detail in the *JavaFX CSS Reference Guide,* which can be found here: https://docs.oracle.com/javase/8/javafx/api/javafx/scene/doc-files/cssref. html. In that document, you can search for a class you need to style and see all applicable CSS properties.

In the preceding example, .root refers to the root element of the scene and .button to all instances of the Button class.

Now, let's use this CSS in the application:

```
// chapter6/basics/FirstStyles.java
public void start(Stage stage) {
    VBox root = new VBox(10);
    Scene scene = new Scene(root, 300, 250);


    Button btnLoad = new Button("Load CSS");
    btnLoad.setOnAction((ActionEvent event) -> {
        // this means take css from the same folder as a current class
scene.getStylesheets().add(getClass().getResource("style.css").toExternalFo
rm());
    });
```

```
    Button btnUnload = new Button("Unoad CSS");
    btnUnload.setOnAction((ActionEvent event) -> {
        scene.getStylesheets().clear();
    });

    root.getChildren().addAll(btnLoad, btnUnload);
    stage.setTitle("Hello CSS!");
    stage.setScene(scene);
    stage.show();
}
```

Text marked in bold dynamically loads a CSS file and applies it to the scene. Without CSS, our app will look as follows:

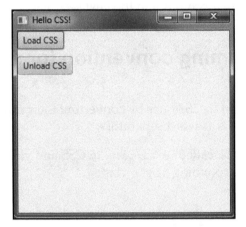

And with CSS, you can see different background colors and padding:

If you are using an IDE, make sure you are running *Clean and Build* after each CSS change as the IDE doesn't always track CSS changes and may not update the output build folder or JAR file.

Matching JavaFX nodes using selectors

Selectors are responsible for matching the style classes you wrote in the CSS file and JavaFX objects. It can be based on a JavaFX class name, specific object ID, or just a style class that is manually assigned to a specific node.

Let's look at each option more thoroughly in the next sections.

Understanding naming convention for style classes and properties

All JavaFX classes are mapped to CSS ones by converting their camel-case names to all lowercase letters with hyphens as word separators.

For example, `GridPane` will be called `grid-pane` in CSS and you can style all `GridPane` objects by adjusting the corresponding `style` class:

```
.grid-pane {
    -fx-background-color: lightblue;
    -fx-padding: 10px;
}
```

This hyphen approach works for properties as well. For example, knowing there is a property named `minWidth`, you can see that the corresponding CSS style property will be named `-fx-min-width`.

There is also a special `.root` style class which refers to any layout manager used in `Scene.setRoot()`.

Also, you can introduce your own style classes and assign them to JavaFX elements manually:

```
// CSS
.blue-style {
    -fx-background-color: lightblue;
}
```

```
// JavaFX
button.getStyleClass().add("blue-style");
```

Note that a node can have several assigned style classes.

Using type selectors

In addition to the previous methods you can address JavaFX elements through the type selectors, using their short class name:

```
GridPane {
    -fx-background-color: lightblue;
    -fx-padding: 10px;
}
```

Here, we are setting the background color and padding properties for all `GridPane` objects that are styled using this CSS.

Styling specific objects using ID selectors

Addressing specific instances of the JavaFX classes can be done with the # symbol:

```
// CSS
#myButton {
    -fx-background-color: lightblue;
}

// JavaFX
Button btn = new Button("hi");
btn.setId("myButton");
```

Here, we style only one instance of the `Button` class, based on the value set in the `setId` method.

Loading CSS files from the JavaFX code

Let's look more thoroughly at the options we have to select a CSS file to load.

The first way is to use the full folder path to the file:

```
scene.getStylesheets().add("/chapter6/basics/style.css");
```

This approach works reliably only if you store your CSS files in a separate resource folder. If your CSS lies along the Java code, any refactoring of the packages may miss this `String` constant. In this case, the better option will be to use a relative path:

```
scene.getStylesheets().add(getClass().getResource("style.css").toExternalFo
rm());
```

By this call, we tell JavaFX to look for `style.css` in the same folder as a current class file.

And the last option is to not store CSS within your project at all but load it from the web:

```
scene.getStylesheets().add("https://raw.githubusercontent.com/sgrinev/maste
ring-javafx-9-10-book/master/Chapter6/src/chapter6/basics/style.css");
```

Although keep in mind that loading CSS happens on the UI thread and the web option in the event of a large CSS or a bad connection will make your whole application freeze for the duration.

Applying styles to JavaFX nodes

Loading a CSS file is not the only option to work with styles. You can also set them directly through an API or specify them in the FXML file. And while this gives additional flexibility, it also requires you to be careful about the priorities of different approaches.

We'll review all the options and see how they interact in the next sections.

Having several CSS files in one JavaFX application

Note that you can use several style sheets simultaneously and apply them not only to `Scene` but to an instance of the class `javafx.scene.Parent` (which most JavaFX nodes are, except primitive shapes).

CSS assigned to a `Parent` will be applied only to this object and all nodes in its children hierarchy.

Using the setStyle() method

The `Node.setStyle(String style)` method can be called directly from the JavaFX code to apply CSS to the given node.

This method is not recommended for use in production applications due to worse performance than other approaches.

But it becomes irreplaceable if you need to build a style on the fly. This approach is very useful for studying styles or trying to find a perfect value for a style.

Let's see it in the example:

```
// chapter6/basics/SetStyleDemo.java
public void start(Stage stage) {
    GridPane root = new GridPane();
    root.setPadding(new Insets(10));
    root.setHgap(5);
    root.setVgap(5);
    Scene scene = new Scene(root, 300, 250);
    TextField fontSize, width, height;

    root.addRow(0, new Label("font size"), fontSize = new TextField("30"));
    root.addRow(1, new Label("width"), width = new TextField("100"));
    root.addRow(2, new Label("height"), height = new TextField("80"));

    Button btnApply = new Button("apply");
    btnApply.setOnAction((e) -> {
        // here we are constructing CSS styles on the fly based on user
values
        btnApply.setStyle(
                "-fx-font-size: " + fontSize.getText() + ";" +
                "-fx-min-width: " + width.getText() + ";" +
                "-fx-min-height: " + height.getText()
                );
    });
    root.add(btnApply, 1, 3);

    stage.setTitle("setStyle Demo");
    stage.setScene(scene);
    stage.show();
}
```

This application starts as follows:

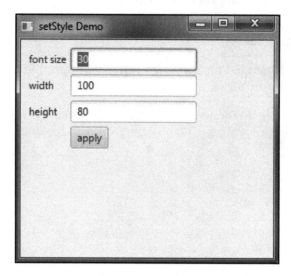

And it looks as follows after click values from text fields are used to create a custom CSS style for a button:

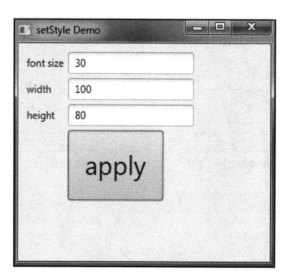

Try it yourself, play with different values in the app and see how it affects the resulting style.

Calling a corresponding API method

Don't forget that instead of CSS `setStyle()`, you can call a corresponding API method. It's the fastest way (performance-wise) to apply a style from Java code because JavaFX doesn't need to spend additional time to parse CSS and style text and then apply the result using Reflection API calls.

The following two methods do the same thing, but the latter one will work faster:

```
btn.setStyle("-fx-min-height: 50");
btn.setMinHeight(50);
```

Referring to CSS styles from FXML

CSS styles and style sheets can be set used in FXML too. We briefly looked at this in `Chapter 4`, *FXML*, while talking about SceneBuilder.

Take a look at the following FXML code and three ways to use styles directly in the FMXL:

```
<!-- Setting a Style Class -->
<Button styleClass="my-button" />

<!-- Setting a style -->
<Button style="-fx-min-height: 50" />

<!-- Setting a whole stylesheet -->
<GridPane stylesheets="@style.css" />
```

Using global JavaFX style sheets

You can use the `Application.setUserAgentStylesheet("/path/to/css")` method to apply CSS files to all Scenes in your application simultaneously.

This method is also used by JavaFX itself to apply default CSS. You can always return to default CSS by calling `Application.setUserAgentStylesheet(null);`.

Currently, there are the following global style sheets by default, accessible by the predefined constants:

```
Application.setUserAgentStylesheet(STYLESHEET_CASPIAN); // JavaFX 2 and
older default style
Application.setUserAgentStylesheet(STYLESHEET_MODENA);  // default style
since JavaFX 8
```

Understanding cascading – the priority scheme for different styling methods

The word *cascading* in the **Cascading Style Sheets** (**CSS**) refers to the priority scheme or order to apply different styles to the one `Node`.

If styles are applied to the `Node` by different means, JavaFX will apply them according to the following rules of priority:

1. A style from `Application.setUserAgentStylesheet()`
2. A value set by an API call such as `btn.setMinHeight(50);`
3. A style from a CSS file set through `Scene.getStylesheets()` or `Parent.getStylesheets()`
4. A style from `Node.setStyle()` overrides all the above items

Thus, `setStyle()` overrides any other style settings. And it really does: once you have changed a property with `setStyle()`, you can't change it by any other means. For example, API calls will be just ignored.

Working with advanced CSS syntax

In this section, we will review the following advanced options:

- Pseudo-classes
- Descendant selectors
- Referring to the resources
- Constants
- The `inherit` keyword

Using pseudo-classes

Pseudo-classes allow you to set different styles for different states of the JavaFX nodes.

For example, for a radio button control, you can set a different style for the selected item using the `:selected` pseudo-class:

```
/* chapter6/syntax/pseudo-class-demo.css */
.radio-button { -fx-font-size: 30 }
.radio-button:selected { -fx-text-fill: red; -fx-font-weight: bold }
```

Using this style sheet in the following demonstration produces a customized radio button group:

```
// chapter6/syntax/PseudoClassDemo.java
public void start(Stage stage) {
    VBox root = new VBox(10);
    ToggleGroup group = new ToggleGroup();
    for (String title : new String[] {"Cats", "Dogs", "Birds", "Mices"}) {
        RadioButton rb = new RadioButton(title);
        rb.setToggleGroup(group);
        root.getChildren().add(rb);
    }

    Scene scene = new Scene(root, 300, 250);
    scene.getStylesheets().add(getClass().getResource("pseudo-class-
demo.css").toExternalForm());
    stage.setTitle("PseudoClass Demo");
    stage.setScene(scene);
    stage.show();
}
```

Note that only the selected button is affected by both `radio-button` (large font) and `radio-button:selected` (bold font) style classes:

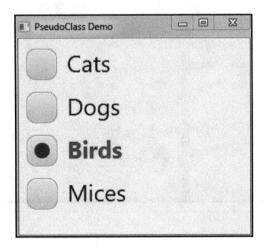

All available pseudo-classes for each node are listed in the JavaFX CSS reference which we discussed at the beginning of the chapter.

Working with descendant selectors

Similar to regular CSS JavaFX supports descendant selectors. You can chain other selectors to limit the scope of the provided style.

Let's slightly enhance the previous example to demonstrate. All the following three styles are applicable to different types of radio buttons in relation to VBox with ID#vb:

```
/* chapter6/syntax/pseudo-class-demo.css */

/* 1. Only direct children of #vb, note the ">" sign */
#vb > .radio-button { -fx-font-size: 20 }
/* 2. All children of #vb */
#vb .radio-button { -fx-underline: true }
/* 3. All radio buttons */
.radio-button:selected { -fx-text-fill: red }
```

To better illustrate this, let's use ScenicView (a very useful JavaFX tool that we discussed in Chapter 2, *Building Blocks – Shapes, Text, and Controls*):

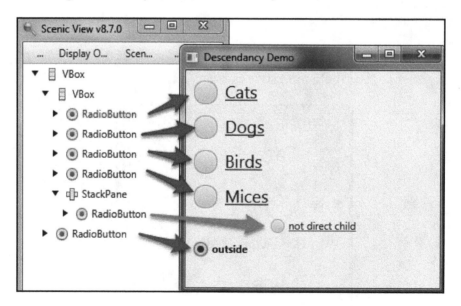

In this screenshot, we can see a SceneGraph and how it affects the applied styles of the similar nodes:

- The top nodes have a large font (item 1 in CSS) and are underlined (item 2) because they are direct children of the #vb node.
- The **not direct child** radio button is affected only by the underline effect (item 2) because it is a child of VBox but not a direct one.
- The **outside** radio button is not affected by items 1 and 2 at all. But as with all radio buttons in this example, it's affected by item 3—bold font on selection.

And here is the code for the preceding screenshot:

```java
// chapter6/syntax/DescendancyDemo.java
public void start(Stage stage) {
    VBox vbox = new VBox(10);
    vbox.setId("vb");
    ToggleGroup group = new ToggleGroup();
    for (String title : new String[] {"Cats", "Dogs", "Birds", "Mices"}) {
        RadioButton rb = new RadioButton(title);
        rb.setToggleGroup(group);
        vbox.getChildren().add(rb);
    }

    RadioButton rbDescendant = new RadioButton("outside");
    rbDescendant.setToggleGroup(group);

    RadioButton rbDeepDescendant = new RadioButton("not direct child");
    rbDeepDescendant.setToggleGroup(group);
    // below we are adding a StackPane to make rbDeepDescendant not a
direct child of VBox
    vbox.getChildren().add(new StackPane(rbDeepDescendant));

    VBox hbox = new VBox(10);
    hbox.getChildren().addAll(vbox, rbDescendant);
    Scene scene = new Scene(hbox, 300, 250);
    scene.getStylesheets().add(getClass().getResource("selectors-
demo.css").toExternalForm());
    stage.setTitle("Descendancy Demo");
    stage.setScene(scene);
    stage.show();
}
```

Working with imports, fonts, and URLs

You can import one CSS from another using the `@import` keyword:

```
@import "style.css";
@import url("http://some-site/style.css");
```

Note the `url` keyword here. You can refer to web resources for things such as cursors or fonts using this keyword.

Talking about fonts, you can use CSS `@font-face` to declare a font in CSS:

```
@font-face {
    font-family: 'myFont';
    font-style: normal;
    font-weight: normal;
    src: url('myfont.ttf');
}
```

Here, `font-family` denotes a name you can now use in CSS or Java code.

Working with constants and the inherit keyword

Currently, only colors can be defined in constants. They are called *looked-up-colors* in the spec:

```
* { my-color: #eee }
.button { -fx-background-color: my-color}
```

This way, you can define a palette for the whole app in one place and easily adjust it.

Another way to reuse styles defined elsewhere is by using the `inherit` keyword. It allows for nested elements to reuse styles defined in parent ones:

```
/* chapter6/syntax/inherit-demo.css */
.root {
    -fx-padding: 10px;
    -fx-background-color: white;
}
.radio-button { -fx-font-size: 30 }
.radio-button:selected > * { -fx-background-color: inherit; }
```

In this example, our radio button will inherit its background color from the parent if selected. This produces the *disappearance* graphical effect. Note that changing the original color will be propagated to the inherited property as well:

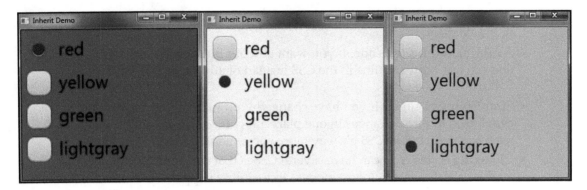

Here is the corresponding code sample:

```
// chapter6/syntax/InheritDemo.java
public void start(Stage stage) {
    VBox root = new VBox(10);
    ToggleGroup group = new ToggleGroup();
    for (String title : new String[] {"red", "yellow", "green",
"lightgray"}) {
        RadioButton rb = new RadioButton(title);
        rb.setToggleGroup(group);
        root.getChildren().add(rb);
    }
    group.selectedToggleProperty().addListener((observable) -> {
        if (group.getSelectedToggle() != null) {
            RadioButton selected = (RadioButton)group.getSelectedToggle();
            root.setStyle("-fx-background-color: " + selected.getText());
        }
    });

    Scene scene = new Scene(root, 300, 250);
    scene.getStylesheets().add(getClass().getResource("inherit-
demo.css").toExternalForm());
    stage.setTitle("Inherit Demo");
    stage.setScene(scene);
    stage.show();
}
```

Why use CSS?

Using CSS over Java code gives you the following benefits:

- **Dividing responsibilities**: You use Java code to write logic and leave all styling to a style sheet.
- **Avoiding duplicated code**: If you want all your buttons to look slightly different, you can just write one line in the CSS instead of adding an API call to each button.
- **Simplifying changes**: If you have changed your mind about that button, you again need to make changes in one place. Of course, this is achievable by Java means as well, but in CSS it's way more convenient.
- **Changing styles**: You can have several CSSes that can be substituted by just one method call. Skins, day/night modes, accessibility support—all these tasks can be addressed by switching style sheets.

Using the CSS API

The CSS API was introduced in JavaFX 8 and extended in JavaFX 9 and 10 with 11 new classes. It's located in the package `javafx.css` and provides the following functionality:

- Make your own styleable properties
- Introduce and support new pseudo-class states

In the following example, we'll add a new style class to control the Clock sample we wrote in the previous chapters.

Introducing ClockControl

Before adding a new style class, let's start by converting out Clock application into a `ClockControl` which can be used in any application like other JavaFX nodes.

It will not be a full-fledged Control, but a first step. We'll talk about making a real Controls in `Chapter 10`, *Advanced Controls and Charts*.

I've made the following changes in order to prepare for CSS handling:

- Made the `ClockControl` class extend `BorderPane`
- Moved all graphics initialization to the `ClockControl` constructor
- Simplified timing logic; the old one was needed to demonstrate the JavaFX API from `Chapter 1`, *Stages, Scenes, and Layout,* and `Chapter 2`, *Building Blocks – Shapes, Text, and Controls.*

The following is the resulting source code:

```java
// chapter6/cssapi/ClockControl.java
public class ClockControl extends BorderPane {

    private final Text txtTime = new Text();
    private final Rotate rotateSecondHand = new Rotate(0, 0, 0);
    private final Rotate rotateMinuteHand = new Rotate(0, 0, 0);
    private final Rotate rotateHourHand = new Rotate(0, 0, 0);
    private final Shape hourHand;

    public ClockControl() {
        // create minutes hand
        Path minuteHand = new Path(
                new MoveTo(0, 0),
                new LineTo(15, -5),
                new LineTo(100, 0),
                new LineTo(15, 5),
                new ClosePath());
        minuteHand.setFill(Color.DARKGRAY);
        minuteHand.getTransforms().add(rotateMinuteHand);
        minuteHand.setTranslateX(minuteHand.getBoundsInLocal().getWidth()/2);

        // create seconds hand
        Line secondHand = new Line(0, 0, 90, 0);
        secondHand.getTransforms().add(rotateSecondHand);
        secondHand.setTranslateX(secondHand.getBoundsInLocal().getWidth()/2);

        // create hours hand
        hourHand = new Path(
                new MoveTo(0, 0),
                new LineTo(20, -8),
                new LineTo(60, 0),
                new LineTo(20, 8),
                new ClosePath());
        hourHand.setFill(Color.LIGHTGRAY);
        hourHand.getTransforms().add(rotateHourHand);
        hourHand.setTranslateX(hourHand.getBoundsInLocal().getWidth() / 2);
```

```
        this.setCenter(new StackPane(minuteHand, hourHand, secondHand));
        this.setBottom(txtTime);
        BorderPane.setAlignment(txtTime, Pos.CENTER);
        Timeline ttimer = new Timeline(new KeyFrame(Duration.seconds(1),
                (event) -> {
                    SimpleDateFormat dt = new SimpleDateFormat("hh:mm:ss");
                    Date now = new Date();
                    String time = dt.format(now);

                    rotateSecondHand.setAngle(now.getSeconds() * 6 - 90);
                    rotateMinuteHand.setAngle(now.getMinutes() * 6 - 90);
                    rotateHourHand.setAngle(now.getHours() * 30 - 90);
                    txtTime.setText(time);
                }));
        ttimer.setCycleCount(Timeline.INDEFINITE);
        ttimer.playFrom(Duration.millis(999));
    }
}
```

Adding a new style class

To make a new style class, we need to perform the following actions:

1. Add StyleableProperty to the property we want to control through CSS.
2. Configure CssMetaData for this property.
3. Expose this metadata through the getCssMetaData() method.

The CssMetaData describes our new styleable property:

- Sets its name, "-fx-hh-color", which will be used in CSS.
- Sets the converter, which will convert strings from CSS into required Java objects. We will use a helper class, PaintConverter, from the javafx.css package. There is a whole range of such converters there.
- Allows read-only mode through the isSettable abstract method. In our example the only thing which may block us is binding, so we will check if the property is bound in this method.
- Links CSS engine to the property we plan to use through the getStyleableProperty method.

Take a look at the following code snippet:

```
private static final CssMetaData<ClockControl, Paint> HH_COLOR_METADATA =
                            new CssMetaData("-fx-hh-color",
PaintConverter.getInstance()) {
        @Override
        public boolean isSettable(Styleable styleable) {
            return !((ClockControl)

            return !((ClockControl) styleable).
                    hourHand.fillProperty().isBound();
        }

        @Override
        public StyleableProperty getStyleableProperty(Styleable styleable)
{
            return ((ClockControl)

            return ((ClockControl) styleable).
                    hourHandColorStyleableProperty;
    };
```

To make a `styleable` property, we'll again use a helper
class, `javafx.css.SimpleStyleableObjectProperty`. It will do all the plumbing for us,
the only thing left to code is updating the color:

```
private SimpleStyleableObjectProperty<Paint> hourHandColorStyleableProperty
=
new SimpleStyleableObjectProperty(HH_COLOR_METADATA) {
        @Override
        protected void invalidated() {
            hourHand.setFill((Paint) get());
        }
    };
```

Now we can inform JavaFX about our new styleable through `getCssMetaData()`:

```
    private static final List<CssMetaData<? extends Styleable, ?>>
cssMetaDataList;
    static {
        List<CssMetaData<? extends Styleable, ?>> temp =
            new ArrayList<>(BorderPane.getClassCssMetaData());
        temp.add(HH_COLOR_METADATA);
        cssMetaDataList = Collections.unmodifiableList(temp);
    }

    @Override
```

```
public List<CssMetaData<? extends Styleable, ?>> getCssMetaData() {
    return cssMetaDataList; }
```

Using the new CSS property

Now we can use our new style class:

```
ClockControl {
    -fx-hh-color: blue;
}
```

We get the following output:

The whole combined source can be found on GitHub. I suggest you experiment with it and try to add more style classes, for example, for the other hands' colors.

Summary

In this chapter, we learned how to use CSS—a powerful mechanism to control and tune the appearance of a JavaFX application. We reviewed CSS syntax, studied the JavaFX specifics of working with CSS, and used the new JavaFX 9 and 10 API to create our own style property.

In the next chapter, we'll study another important aspect of the modern application—building a dynamic UI.

Building a Dynamic UI

7

In this chapter, we will take a break from studying JavaFX APIs and look into good practices for using them.

Modern applications are not set in stone and try to adapt to different users' settings, most prominently the size of the application's window. This may change due to a variety of reasons: different devices, rotation, split-screen functionality, or just the user's manual resizing to a comfortable position. This adaptivity, or a dynamic UI, provides a better user experience.

We will review the following practices for building a dynamic UI:

- Tuning `min` and `max` size properties
- Controlling node location with AnchorPane
- Planning node size behavior with grow priorities
- Fluid layouts
- Enhancing applications with scrolling

Tuning min and max size properties

JavaFX provides a convenient approach to component sizes with properties: min, preferred, and max. These values are used by layout managers to represent their children.

Let's take a button, for example. A button's width is governed by the length of the text inside; on the other hand, a button can't outgrow its container so text may be shortened if there is not enough space—these are natural constraints, but you can impose extra ones by setting `setMinWidth()` and `setMaxWidth()`.

Let's see in code how different size constraints work in JavaFX:

```java
// chapter7/resising/MinMaxSizeDemo.java
Button btnNoMin = new Button("I have no min width");

Button btnMin = new Button("I have min width");
btnMin.setMinWidth(100);

Button btnMax = new Button("I have limited max width");
btnMax.setMaxWidth(140);

Button btnBig = new Button("I have large max width");
btnBig.setMaxWidth(1000);

Button btnBig2 = new Button("me too");
btnBig2.setMaxWidth(1000);
VBox root = new VBox(5);
root.setPadding(new Insets(20));
root.getChildren().addAll(btnNoMin, btnMin, btnMax, btnBig, btnBig2);
```

The following screenshot shows the buttons' reactions to the different window sizes:

Note how setting minimal width allows us to keep a certain part of the text visible for as long as possible. And setting a large value as a maximum width for the two bottom buttons made them keep the same width while being resized.

Controlling node location with AnchorPane

AnchorPane is a powerful tool for fine-tuning the resize process. It allows us to precisely attach nodes to the four sides of the window.

Imagine we are creating a browser that consists of the following components:

- An address bar
- Navigation buttons
- A status bar
- A web view:

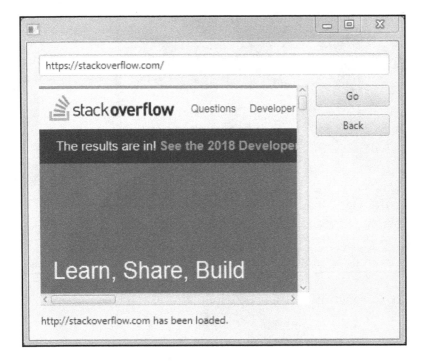

If the browser is being resized, we want the following adaptive behavior:

- The address bar stays on top and changes size only in the horizontal direction
- Same for the status bar, but in the bottom
- The web view is the most important part and should take as much space as possible
- Buttons shouldn't resize at all, but we want them to stay at the same location

To achieve that, we put them all into `AnchorPane` and attach them to its borders correspondingly:

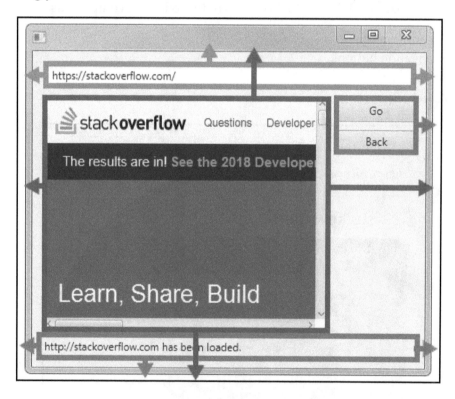

One way is to do it through an API, as in the following example:

```
AnchorPane root = new AnchorPane();
TextField addressAtTop = new TextField("www.stackoverflow.com");
AnchorPane.setTopAnchor(addressAtTop, 10.);
AnchorPane.setLeftAnchor(addressAtTop, 10.);
AnchorPane.setRightAnchor(addressAtTop, 10.);
```

But it's way more convenient to do it in FXML using the ScenicView tool we discussed in Chapter 4, *FXML* (note that I've removed all unrelated code to make this more readable; for the full sample, look at the GitHub file):

```
<!-- chapter7/resising/browser/browser.fxml -->

<AnchorPane prefHeight="324.0" prefWidth="380.0">
    <children>
        <WebView AnchorPane.bottomAnchor="40.0" AnchorPane.leftAnchor="14.0"
                 AnchorPane.rightAnchor="110.0" AnchorPane.topAnchor="51.0"/>
        <TextField text="http://stackoverflow.com" layoutX="14.0"
layoutY="14.0"
                 AnchorPane.leftAnchor="14.0" AnchorPane.rightAnchor="11.0"/>
        <Button   AnchorPane.topAnchor="51.0" AnchorPane.rightAnchor="11.0"
                  prefWidth="90.0" text="Go" />
        <Button   AnchorPane.topAnchor="85.0" AnchorPane.rightAnchor="11.0"
                  prefWidth="90.0" text="Back" />
        <Label    AnchorPane.bottomAnchor="14.0" AnchorPane.leftAnchor="14.0"
                  AnchorPane.rightAnchor="11.0" text="Status Text" />
    </children>
</AnchorPane>
```

Now let's look at a resized application window that has followed all the rules we've set:

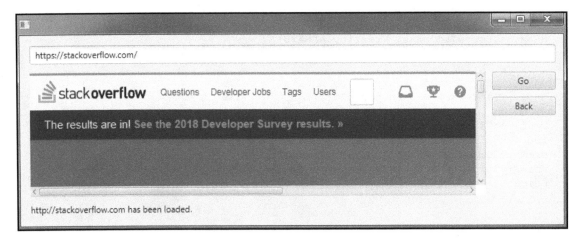

Planning node size behavior with grow priorities

For simpler layout managers, such as HBox, you can also control how nodes behave under pressure.

For example, let's look at the browser address bar again: there are some buttons on the left, a text field for the address, and some buttons on the right—but we want only the address box to change size:

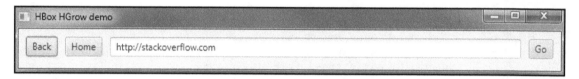

API methods for that are static and called `setHgrow()` for HBox and `setVgrow()` for VBox. GridPane has both of them too. For some reason, they are static and their usage looks as follows:

```
// chapter7/resizing/HGrowDemo.java
HBox root = new HBox(10);
TextField address = new TextField("http://stackoverflow.com");
HBox.setHgrow(address, Priority.ALWAYS);

root.getChildren().addAll(
        new Button("Back"), new Button("Home");
        address, new Button("Go"));

root.setPadding(new Insets(10));
root.setAlignment(Pos.TOP_LEFT);
primaryStage.setTitle("HBox HGrow demo");
primaryStage.setScene(new Scene(root, 350, 50));
primaryStage.show();
```

Using static methods may be tricky in FXML, so here is an example:

```
<HBox prefHeight="100.0" prefWidth="200.0">
    <children>
        <Button text="Back" />
        <Button text="Home" />
        <TextField HBox.hgrow="ALWAYS" />
        <Button text="Go" />
    </children>
</HBox>
```

Fluid layouts

Despite all the listed practices, you can only shrink elements so much. So the next option will be to rearrange them once space becomes a bigger issue.

The easiest thing to adapt is text. It can be naturally split into words into separate lines saving width at the price of height. Most controls which contain text support `wrapText` property to control that behavior.

Default button behavior is to show ellipses (...) if the text is too long. It can be changed using `wrapTextProperty()` value:

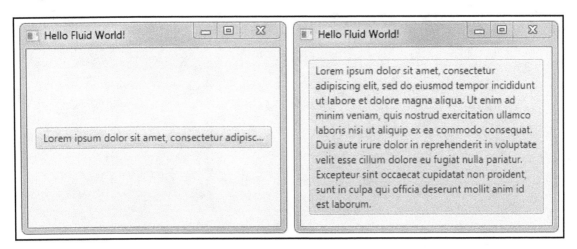

For other nodes, similar behavior is provided by the FlowPane layout manager.

Note that it doesn't work ideally for all configurations and fluid UI structure may confuse users. Property pages are one convenient example, as shown in the following screenshot:

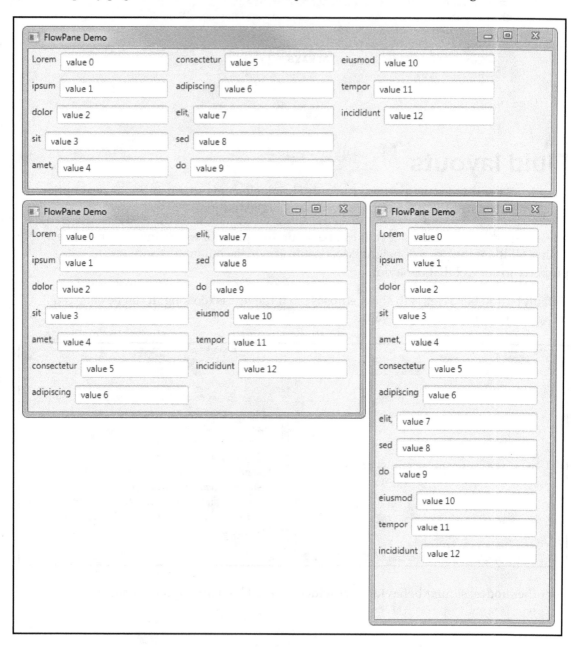

To create such a UI, we use `FlowPane` and populate it with properties:

```
// chapter7/resizing/FlowLayoutDemo.java
FlowPane root = new FlowPane();
root.setOrientation(Orientation.VERTICAL);

// generating "properties"
int rnd = 0;
for (String string : "Lorem ipsum dolor sit amet, consectetur adipiscing
elit, sed do eiusmod tempor incididunt".split(" ")) {
    TextField tf = new TextField("value " + rnd++);
    HBox.setHgrow(tf, Priority.ALWAYS); // to make it look better
    HBox hBox = new HBox(5, new Label(string), tf);
    hBox.setPadding(new Insets(5));
    root.getChildren().add(hBox);
}
primaryStage.setTitle("FlowPane Demo");
primaryStage.setScene(new Scene(root, 450, 250));
primaryStage.show();
```

Enhancing applications with scrolling

We shouldn't omit a common but powerful way to present large chunks of information in smaller areas—scrolling.

In JavaFX, a `ScrollPane` layout manager provides a scrollable, clipped viewport of its content. Usage is conveniently simple—you can put any node or layout manager into ScrollPane using the `setContent()` method.

For example, let's put content from our previous sample into `ScrollPane`:

```
// chapter7/resizing/ScrollPaneDemo.java
FlowPane pane = new FlowPane();
pane.setOrientation(Orientation.VERTICAL);
ScrollPane root = new ScrollPane();
root.setContent(pane);
```

In the following screenshot, you can see the resulting scrollable view:

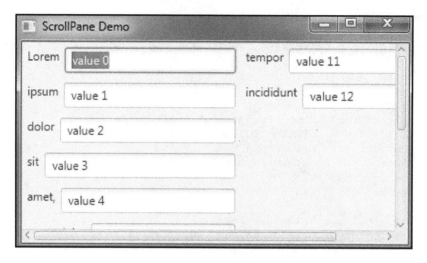

Summary

In this chapter, we reviewed various ways to provide a good user experience for different window sizes using JavaFX. Modern users are quite demanding with regard to user interfaces and want comfortable and easy-to-use applications.

Continuing in this direction, in the next chapter, we'll get back to our API review and will look into various visual effects, and how we can use them to make our applications more appealing.

8
Effects

Modern users are used to extra eye candy in their UI. JavaFX provides a wide range of various effects to provide great-looking UI elements.

In this chapter, we will cover the following topics related to the Effects API:

- Basic effects: shadows, reflections, and blur
- Combining effects
- Color effects
- Lighting effects
- Transformation effects
- Blend modes

Applying basic effects

All effects can be applied to any `Node` on the SceneGraph through the `effectProperty()` and corresponding `Node.setEffect(Effect value)` methods.

Adding shadow effects

Shadows are one of the oldest effects. They were used to imitate three dimensions on a flat paper surface even before the advent of computers. In the next sections, we will review the different types of shadow provided by the JavaFX Effects API.

Using DropShadow

The `javafx.scene.effect.DropShadow` effect is a shadow which imitates different light source locations, and is drawn outside the shadowed node, as in the following example:

To add `DropShadow`, you just need to instantiate a corresponding class with the desired parameters:

```
// chapter8/basiceffects/DropShadowDemo.java
public void start(Stage stage) throws Exception {
    Circle red = new Circle(50, Color.RED);
    red.setEffect(new DropShadow());

    Circle yellow = new Circle(50, Color.YELLOW);
    yellow.setEffect(new DropShadow(
            10,        // shadow radius
            10, 0,     // x,y offset
            Color.DARKGRAY));

    Circle green = new Circle(50, Color.GREEN);
    green.setEffect(new DropShadow(10, 10, 10, Color.DARKGRAY));

    VBox root = new VBox(10, red, yellow, green);
    root.setAlignment(Pos.CENTER);
    stage.setScene(new Scene(root, 200, 350));
    stage.show();
}
```

Note that `Effect` may change the visual size of the `Node`, but from the layout point of view, it wouldn't change the location of the original nodes. So `Node` objects may now visually intersect, but will still be laid out by the original borders.

This is another example of different node borders we talked about in Chapter 2, *Building Blocks – Shapes, Text, and Controls*. Original bounds are described by `node.getLayoutBounds()` and actual ones with effects (and transformations) can be found by `node.getBoundsInParent()`:

Using InnerShadow

The `InnerShadow` effect imitates external lighting by drawing a shadow inside the node:

Similar to `DropShadow`, this effect is controlled by corresponding class constructor parameters. Take a look at the following code:

```java
// chapter8/basiceffects/InnerShadowDemo.java
Circle red = new Circle(50, Color.RED);
red.setEffect(new InnerShadow());

Circle yellow = new Circle(50, Color.YELLOW);
yellow.setEffect(new InnerShadow(
        10,     // shadow radius
        10, 0, // x,y offset
        Color.BLACK));

Circle green = new Circle(50, Color.GREEN);
green.setEffect(new InnerShadow(10, 10, 10, Color.BLACK));
```

Understanding the base Shadow effect

The base `Shadow` effect produces an output which looks like a node shadow, but without the original node:

The code is again very simple:

```java
public void start(Stage stage) throws Exception {
    Circle circle = new Circle(50, Color.RED);
    circle.setEffect(new Shadow());
    stage.setScene(new Scene(new StackPane(circle), 200, 350));
    stage.show();
}
```

Adding reflections

Another simple but powerful effect is `Reflection`.

The API is straightforward:

```
// chapter8/basiceffects/ReflectionDemo.java
public void start(Stage primaryStage) {
    Reflection reflection = new Reflection();
    reflection.setTopOffset(5);   // how far from source the reflection
should start
    reflection.setFraction(0.7); // size of the reflection
    // starting and ending opacity levels
    reflection.setTopOpacity(0.05);
    reflection.setBottomOpacity(0.5);

    Button button = new Button("Button");
    button.setEffect(reflection);

    primaryStage.setTitle("Reflection Demo");
    primaryStage.setScene(new Scene(new StackPane(button), 300, 250));
    primaryStage.show();
}
```

The preceding code produces the following:

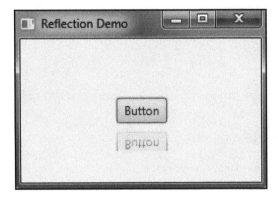

Combining effects

By combining just reflection and shadow effects, you can already achieve nice-looking elements, for example:

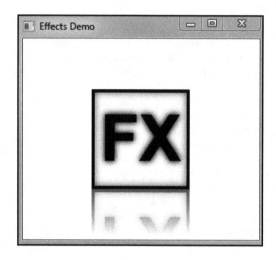

Refer to the following code snippet:

```
// chapter8/combining/ReflectionAndShadows.java
public void start(Stage stage) {
    // outer rectangle has a inner shadow
    Rectangle rect = new Rectangle(120, 120);
    rect.setFill(Color.WHITE);
    rect.setStroke(Color.BLACK);
    rect.setStrokeWidth(4);
    rect.setEffect(new InnerShadow(15, Color.BLACK));

    // text has a drop shadow
    Text text = new Text("FX");
    text.setFont(Font.font("Arial", FontWeight.BOLD, 80));
    text.setEffect(new DropShadow());

    // to apply reflection to both
    // we need to have a common node
    StackPane square = new StackPane(rect, text);
    // this way our StackPane will be small
    // and just wrap the rectangle
    square.setMaxSize(0, 0);

    // aplying reflection
```

```
    Reflection reflection = new Reflection();
    reflection.setFraction(0.45);
    square.setEffect(reflection);

    StackPane root = new StackPane(square);
    stage.setTitle("Effects Demo");
    stage.setScene(new Scene(root, 300, 250));
    stage.show();
}
```

Another option to combine effects is setting one effect as an input for another with the setInput() method:

```
public void start(Stage primaryStage) {
    Rectangle rect1 = new Rectangle(50, 50, Color.RED);
    DropShadow effect1 = new DropShadow();
    effect1.setInput(new Reflection());
    rect1.setEffect(effect1);

    Rectangle rect2 = new Rectangle(50, 50, Color.RED);
    Reflection effect2 = new Reflection();
    effect2.setInput(new DropShadow());
    rect2.setEffect(effect2);

    HBox root = new HBox(30, rect1, rect2);
    root.setPadding(new Insets(50));
    primaryStage.setTitle("Inputs");
    primaryStage.setScene(new Scene(root, 230, 200));
    primaryStage.show();
}
```

You can chain any number of effects this way. But you need to be careful about the order. The preceding example will produce two different outputs for the same effects applied in a different order:

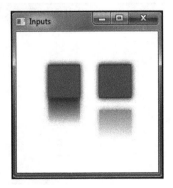

The thing is that each effect changes the actual size of the Node (`boundsInParent`) and the next one will use this new size and produce a different result.

Another option for combining effects is blending, which we will review in the *Using blend effects* section.

Distorting using blur effects

There are three different types of blur you can use to distort parts of the UI: `GaussianBlur`, `MotionBlur`, and `BoxBlur`:

```
public void start(Stage primaryStage) {
    Button btn = new Button("Gaussian Blur");
    btn.setEffect(new GaussianBlur(3));
    Button btn2 = new Button("Motion Blur");
    btn2.setEffect(new MotionBlur(0, 10));
    Button btn3 = new Button("Box Blur");
    btn3.setEffect(new BoxBlur());

    VBox vbox = new VBox(30, btn, btn2, btn3);
    vbox.setPadding(new Insets(50));
    primaryStage.setTitle("Blurry Demo");
    primaryStage.setScene(new Scene(vbox, 300, 250));
    primaryStage.show();
}
```

As you can see in the following screenshot, the `MotionBlur` effect tried to imitate the look of a moving object. `GaussianBlur` and `BoxBlur` are pretty similar; just choose one by its appearance.

Here is an example of all three blur effects in action:

Adding color effects

A whole range of color effects produces results similar to the Instagram filters from Instagram. In upcoming sections, we will look at the following color effects:

- `ColorAdjust`
- `ColorInput`
- `SepiaTone`
- `Bloom`
- `Glow`

Using ColorAdjust

The `ColorAdjust` effect allows us to change the following properties of any node (usually, it is applied to images):

- Hue
- Brightness
- Contrast
- Saturation

Refer to the following screenshot:

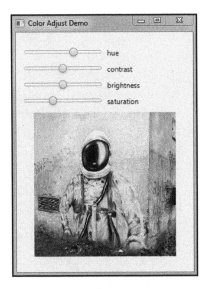

You can really only see how it works in action, so I advise you to run the following sample and try the corresponding controls:

```
// chapter8/colors/ColorAdjustDemo
public void start(Stage primaryStage) {
    // you can use any local image here, I've just provided web one to
simplify project stucture
    ImageView iv = new
ImageView("https://raw.githubusercontent.com/sgrinev/mastering-javafx-9-10-
book/master/resources/sample.jpg");
    iv.setFitHeight(240);
    iv.setFitWidth(240);
    ColorAdjust ca = new ColorAdjust();
    iv.setEffect(ca);

    VBox root = new VBox(10);
    for (DoubleProperty prop : new DoubleProperty[] {
        ca.hueProperty(), ca.contrastProperty(), ca.brightnessProperty(),
ca.saturationProperty()
    }) {
        Slider slider = new Slider(-1, 1, 0.);
        prop.bind(slider.valueProperty());
        root.getChildren().add(new HBox(5, slider, new
Label(prop.getName())));
    }
    root.getChildren().add(iv);
    root.setAlignment(Pos.CENTER);
    root.setPadding(new Insets(10));

    primaryStage.setTitle("Color Adjust Demo");
    primaryStage.setScene(new Scene(root, 300, 400));
    primaryStage.show();
}
```

A popular question is how to use `ColorAdjust` to convert an image into a monochrome one. You can achieve that by setting the saturation to -1: `ca.setSaturation(-1);`

Using ColorInput

This effect is not used by itself, but only as an input for other effects. It produces a rectangular area filled with the given color:

```
ColorInput effect = new ColorInput(0, 0, 100, 50, Color.RED);
```

Using SepiaTone

Sepia is a popular photo filter which gives a reddish-brown tone to a photo to make it look like an old photograph from the pre-digital era.

It has only one property: `levelProperty`, with a range from 0 to 1. Take a look at the following code snippet:

```
//  chapter8/colors/SepiaToneDemo.java
SepiaTone st = new SepiaTone();
st.setLevel(0.5);
imageView.setEffect(st):
```

Bloom and Glow

Both `Bloom` and `Glow` provide a glowing effect based on the color of the Node:

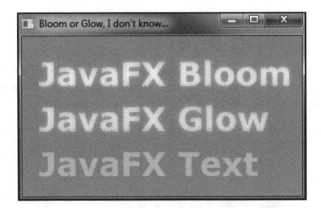

The difference is pretty subtle. You can try to spot it yourself by toying with the code:

```
// chapter8/colors/BloomGlowDemo.java
public void start(Stage primaryStage) {
    Function<String,Text> makeLabel = (String name)-> {
        Text label = new Text(name);
        label.setFill(Color.LIGHTBLUE);
        label.setFont(Font.font("Verdana", FontWeight.BOLD, 40));
        return label;
    };
```

```
Text label = makeLabel.apply("JavaFX Bloom");
label.setEffect(new Bloom(0.8));

Text label2 = makeLabel.apply("JavaFX Glow");
label2.setEffect(new Glow(0.8));

Text label3 = makeLabel.apply("JavaFX Text");

VBox root = new VBox(5, label, label2, label3);
root.setPadding(new Insets(20));
root.setBackground(Background.EMPTY);

Scene scene = new Scene(root, 400, 250, Color.DARKGRAY);

primaryStage.setTitle("Bloom or Glow, I don't know...");
primaryStage.setScene(scene);
primaryStage.show();
}
```

Applying lighting effects

Lighting is a complex effect dedicated to giving an object pseudo-3D depth by imitating a light source. An algorithm finds node boundaries and graphically elevates them by shading those further from the imaginary light and lighting the closer ones:

To achieve this effect, you'll have to set the location and type of an *imaginary light*, which shines on the scene and is implemented as shown in the following code snippet:

```
// chapter8/light/LightingDemo.java
public void start(Stage primaryStage) {
    Light.Distant light = new Light.Distant();
    light.setAzimuth(-135);

    Lighting lighting = new Lighting();
    lighting.setLight(light);
    lighting.setSurfaceScale(5);

    Text text = new Text("FX");
    text.setFill(Color.STEELBLUE);
    text.setFont(Font.font(null, FontWeight.BOLD, 70));

    text.setEffect(lighting);

    Rectangle rect = new Rectangle(70, 70, Color.LIGHTGREEN);
    rect.setEffect(lighting); // note we can reuse the effect object

    Circle circle = new Circle(60, Color.TRANSPARENT);
    circle.setStroke(Color.DARKGRAY);
    circle.setStrokeWidth(10);
    circle.setEffect(lighting);

    HBox root = new HBox(10, text, rect, circle);
    root.setAlignment(Pos.CENTER);
    root.setPadding(new Insets(20));
    Scene scene = new Scene(root, 400, 150);

    primaryStage.setTitle("Lighting Demo");
    primaryStage.setScene(scene);
    primaryStage.show();
}
```

Understanding the types of light

There are three types of light source: Distant, Spot, and Point. They all extend the base abstract class `Light`. A common property for all light types is a color. Note that, despite having a 2D scene, `Light` requires the third coordinate to locate an imaginary light source.

Using Distant light

The `Light.Distant` class imitates sunlight coming from a large distance, which you control only by the direction, set by elevation and direction (called the azimuth) angles, measured in degrees. The azimuth's boundaries are 0 and 360, and the elevation's boundaries range from 0 to 90:

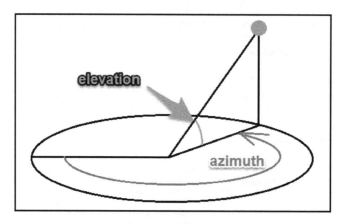

The sample of the preceding `LightingDemo` on GitHub has controls to adjust both angles to see how it works for different values:

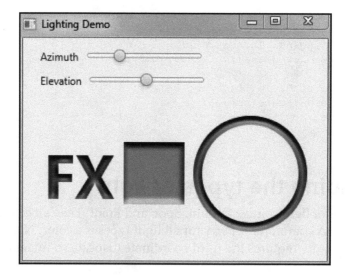

Using Spot light

The `Light.Spot` class imitates a real-life spotlight—you can choose its location, the direction, and the light style and JavaFX will apply the corresponding lighting to your nodes.

The actual results are easier to understand in a dynamic form, so I've prepared a demonstration that allows all parameters to be tweaked:

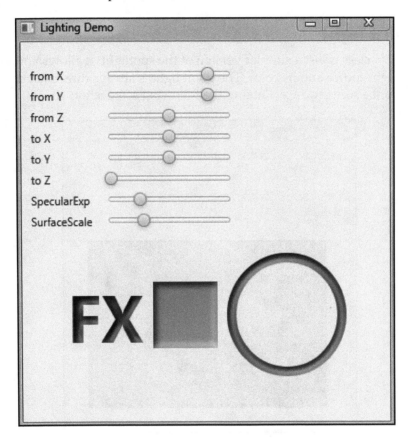

Its listing is too long for the book; please find it on the book's GitHub. I'll provide only spotlight creation here:

```
// chapter8/light/SpotLightDemo.java
Light.Spot light = new Light.Spot(200, 150, 500, 1, Color.WHITE);
light.setPointsAtX(100);
light.setPointsAtY(100);
light.setPointsAtZ(0);
```

Using Point light

The `Light.Point` class is just a simpler version of the spotlight. It allows you to set the location of the light source and its color. The point light is always directed *down*, perpendicular to the scene surface. Refer to the following screenshot:

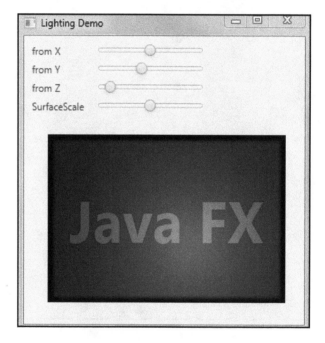

Here is part of the sample, related to the created effect:

```
Light.Point light = new Light.Point(200, 150, 100, Color.WHITE);
Lighting lighting = new Lighting();
lighting.setLight(light);
lighting.setSurfaceScale(5.0);

Text text = new Text("Java FX");
```

```
text.setFill(Color.STEELBLUE);
text.setFont(Font.font(null, FontWeight.BOLD, 70));
Rectangle rect = new Rectangle(300, 200, Color.BLUE);

StackPane items = new StackPane(rect, text);
items.setEffect(lighting);
```

Using BumpInput

An important lighting parameter is `SurfaceScale`, which determines how *high* the border should be elevated for the sake of light imitation. You saw how it affects the result in the preceding examples.

But you can choose what to elevate exactly by using the `setBumpInput(Effect input)` method. Technically, you can use any effect as a bump map here, but most convenient will be `ImageInput`. In the selected image, transparent areas will stay flat and everything else will be elevated and highlighted.

In the following example, the Packt logo was used as an `ImageInput`:

I've highlighted the most important parts of the code:

```
//chapter8/light/BumpInputDemo.java

// initialize light effect
Light.Distant light = new Light.Distant();
light.setAzimuth(100);
light.setElevation(45);

// image for bump input
ImageInput ii = new ImageInput(new
Image("https://raw.githubusercontent.com/sgrinev/mastering-javafx-9-10-book
/master/resources/sample.jpg"), 0, 70); // 70 here is a vertical offset

// create lighting and set bump input
Lighting lighting = new Lighting();
lighting.setLight(light);
lighting.setBumpInput(ii);

// node which we apply effect to
ImageView iv = new ImageView(new
Image("https://raw.githubusercontent.com/sgrinev/mastering-javafx-9-10-book
/master/resources/sample.jpg", 250, 250, true, true));
iv.setEffect(lighting);
```

Transformation effects

These effects distort the shape of the node, usually to imitate physical effects, for example, perspective or water waves.

These effects require quite a few parameters to set up and a bit of math is involved.

Setting up PerspectiveTransform

The `PerspectiveTransform` effect is another effect which tries to simulate 3D. It changes the node's dimensions so it appears to be viewed not from the top to the bottom but at an angle.

The API is slightly awkward—you need to set all four corners of the new image by setting eight coordinates by different method calls:

```
// chapter8/geometry/PerspectiveDemo.java
PerspectiveTransform pt = new PerspectiveTransform();
```

```
pt.setUlx(20);   // upper-left
pt.setUly(20);
pt.setUrx(100); // upper-right
pt.setUry(20);

pt.setLlx(0);    // lower-left
pt.setLly(120);
pt.setLrx(120); // lower-right
pt.setLry(120);
```

Or use a very long constructor:

```
PerspectiveTransform pt = new PerspectiveTransform(20, 20, 100, 20, 0,
120, 120, 120);
```

I've marked each corner on the following screenshot for convenience:

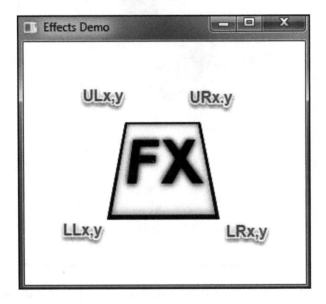

 Don't forget that all effects are purely cosmetic. So all bounds, containment, and mouse hit methods will use original, untransformed coordinates. If you need to transform something more functional—for example, buttons—it is better to opt for the Transformations API we talked about in Chapter 2, *Building Blocks – Shapes, Text, and Controls*.

Distorting an image with DisplacementMap

The DisplacementMap effect is a pretty complex effect and takes transformations to the next level. Instead of only four corners, as in PerspectiveTransform, you can set up adjustments for each pixel of the original node. But creating a nice effect from scratch will require some math knowledge.

Let's look at the logic that adds the following wavy effect to an image we used previously in the chapter:

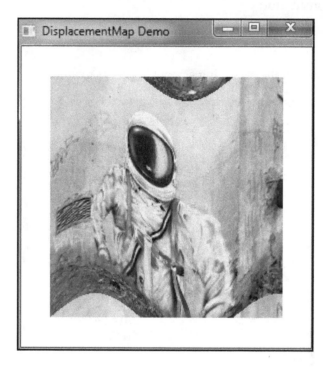

To shift like that, we will use the sine function and move all pixels only in vertical directions following the sine's values.

To set up DisplacementMap, you need to add coordinate correction data for each pixel in the FloatMap helper class:

```
FloatMap floatMap = new FloatMap();

// ...
floatMap.setSamples(x, y, shiftX, shiftY);
```

Here, we are moving the pixel at the (*x*,*y*) coordinates by (shiftX, shiftY), where shift values are a percentage of the image size. For example, shift=0 will leave a pixel in place and shift=1 will move it from one side of the picture to another. Here is how it will look for our sine example:

```
// chapter8/geometry/DisplacementMapDemo.java
final int SIDE = 240;
ImageView iv = new
ImageView("https://raw.githubusercontent.com/sgrinev/mastering-javafx-9-10-
book/master/resources/sample.jpg");
iv.setFitHeight(SIDE);
iv.setFitWidth(SIDE);

FloatMap floatMap = new FloatMap();
floatMap.setWidth(SIDE);
floatMap.setHeight(SIDE);

for (int x = 0; x < SIDE; x++) {
    double v = Math.sin( x / 30. ) / 10.;
    for (int y = 0; y < SIDE; y++) {
        floatMap.setSamples(x, y, 0.0f, (float)v);
    }
}

DisplacementMap displacementMap = new DisplacementMap();
displacementMap.setWrap(true);
displacementMap.setMapData(floatMap);
iv.setEffect(displacementMap);
```

Note that pixels that we moved outside the image border appeared on the other side. It's controlled by the `displacementMap.setWrap(true)` method.

Using blend effects

Blending is a way to merge two inputs with different modes. The input can be a `ColorInput`, an image, or a regular node. There are 17 different modes of merging. It's hard to find a use case for all of them so I will review only the most often used subset.

Cutting out with the SRC_ATOP blend mode

This blend mode draws only part of the top input lying inside the node it's applied to. By using this, you can get nice clipping effect:

Here, we used the same cosmonaut image as a fill for the "JavaFX" text:

```
// chapter8/combining/BlendSrcDemo.java
public void start(Stage primaryStage) {
    Image image = new Image(
"https://github.com/sgrinev/mastering-javafx-9-book/blob/master/resources/s
ample.jpg?raw=true",
        300, 300, true, true);
    ImageInput ii = new ImageInput(image, 0, 0);

    Blend blend = new Blend();
    blend.setMode(BlendMode.SRC_ATOP);
    blend.setTopInput(ii);

    Text text = new Text(0, 80, "JavaFX");
    text.setFont(Font.font("Verdana", FontWeight.BOLD, 70));
    text.setEffect(blend);

    primaryStage.setTitle("Blend Demo");
    primaryStage.setScene(new Scene(new StackPane(text), 300, 300));
    primaryStage.show();
}
```

Calculating the difference between images

This BlendMode highlights the difference between two nodes (usually images):

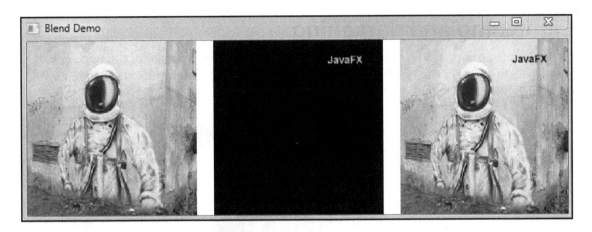

You need to use one image as an input and another as an effect's target:

```
// chapter8/combining/BlendDiffDemo.java
public void start(Stage primaryStage) {
    Image image = new Image(
"https://github.com/sgrinev/mastering-javafx-9-book/blob/master/resources/s
ample.jpg?raw=true",
        200, 200, true, true);
    ImageInput ii = new ImageInput(image, 0, 0);

    Image image2 = new Image(
"https://github.com/sgrinev/mastering-javafx-9-book/blob/master/resources/s
ample2.jpg?raw=true",
        200, 200, true, true);

    Blend blend = new Blend();
    blend.setMode(BlendMode.DIFFERENCE);
    blend.setTopInput(ii);

    ImageView iv = new ImageView(image2);
    iv.setEffect(blend);

    primaryStage.setTitle("Blend Demo");
    primaryStage.setScene(new Scene(
        new HBox(20, new ImageView(image), iv, new ImageView(image2)), 640,
200));
    primaryStage.show();
}
```

Lightening and darkening

The BlendMode chooses the lighter (or darker, respectively) component of the two sources and uses it to produce the result. In the following screenshot, both inputs are blended with the same white-to-black gradient:

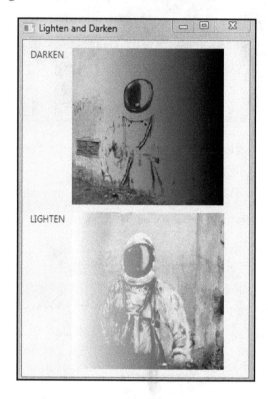

The code is pretty similar, but note we are using ColorInput for the first time in this book:

```
// chapter8/combining/LightAndDarkDemo.java
public void start(Stage primaryStage) {
    VBox root = new VBox(10);
    root.setPadding(new Insets(10));
    final Image image = new
Image("https://raw.githubusercontent.com/sgrinev/mastering-javafx-9-10-book
/master/resources/sample.jpg", 200, 200, true, true);

    Stop[] stops = new Stop[]{new Stop(0, Color.WHITE), new Stop(1,
Color.BLACK)};
    LinearGradient gradient = new LinearGradient(0, 0, 1, 0, true,
CycleMethod.NO_CYCLE, stops);
```

```
        ColorInput ci = new ColorInput(0, 0, 200, 200, gradient);

        for (BlendMode value : new BlendMode[] { BlendMode.DARKEN,
BlendMode.LIGHTEN}) {
            Blend blend = new Blend();
            blend.setMode(value);

            blend.setTopInput(ci);
            ImageView iv = new ImageView(image);
            iv.setEffect(blend);

            root.getChildren().add(new HBox(10, new Label(value.toString()),
iv));
        }

        primaryStage.setTitle("Lighten and Darken");
        primaryStage.setScene(new Scene(root,300, 430));
        primaryStage.show();
    }
```

Other blend modes

There are 14 more blend modes in JavaFX 10. I've combined them all in a demonstation in the `chapter8/combining/AllBlendModesDemo.java` file on GitHub. Take a look and play with various sources to get a better grasp of blending.

Summary

We reviewed a lot of effects in this chapter. Note that some of them are already used in the JavaFX controls so you are not always obliged to add them to have a modern-looking application. Also, not all effects are eye candy: `Blend`, `Lighting`, `ColorAdjust`, and others are powerful tools to create interesting functionality.

In the next chapter, we will look at integrating our applications with external content through the powerful Media and WebView components.

Media and WebView

9

In this chapter, we will learn how to incorporate audio, video, and web content into a JavaFX application.

We will cover the following topics:

- Adding web content using `WebView` and `WebEngine`
- Working with the Document Object Model and JavaScript from JavaFX
- Adding audio clips and songs
- Adding video content
- Adding effects to video content

Working with web content

The `WebView` component is a component that can render modern HTML pages. It's based on WebKit (`https://webkit.org/`), an open-source browser engine that is widely used.

WebView consists of two parts:

- `WebView` itself, which is a JavaFX node and can be used in SceneGraph
- The `WebEngine` class, which is responsible for all HTML and JavaScript logic

Technically, there is also a third component—a rendering engine. It's not provided by WebKit and JavaFX has its own. But developers usually do not communicate with it.

Presenting web content with WebView

Let's look at a simple `WebView` example:

```
// chapter9/web/WebViewDemo.java
public void start(Stage primaryStage) {
    WebView wv = new WebView();
    wv.getEngine().load("https://stackoverflow.com/questions/tagged/javafx");

    StackPane root = new StackPane(wv);
    primaryStage.setTitle("JavaFX on SO");
    primaryStage.setScene(new Scene(root, 400, 250));
    primaryStage.show();
}
```

This loads and shows a page from `stackoverflow.com`:

In the next section, let's look at useful properties of `WebView`: the context menu and accessibility features.

Context menu

Setting the `contextMenuEnabled` property to `true` will enable a context menu with some basic functions in `WebView`:

It provides some basic operations, such as opening links, reloading, and working with a clipboard. But there is no API to control it in any way, so the usefulness of this menu is limited.

Note that the **Open Link in New Window** functionality requires setting a pop-up handler as described in the *Loading content and user interface callbacks* section.

Accessibility features

You can also control the font size or zoom in `WebView`:

```
webView.setZoom(1.2);          // +20%
webView.setFontScale(1.5);     // +50%
```

But note that the font scaled here is on the JavaFX rendering level, which means that web page layouts and styles will be distorted.

Web engine

The rest of the functionality one may expect from the WebView API is provided by WebEngine, most importantly access to the JavaScript and HTML document of the represented web page.

Handling page loading progress with LoadWorker

The `WebEngine.getLoadWorker()` method returns a `Worker` object that tracks the progress of the page loading.

The most important properties of `Worker` are the following:

- `progressProperty`: This represents the page loading progress
- `stateProperty`: This represents the status of the loading process, especially `Worker.State.FAILED` and `Worker.State.SUCCEEDED`

In the next example, we will use these properties to add a progress loading indicator and messages about the end of the page loading:

```java
// chapter9/web/LoadWorkerDemo.java
public void start(Stage primaryStage) {
    WebView webView = new WebView();
    WebEngine webEngine = webView.getEngine();
    webEngine.load("https://stackoverflow.com/questions/tagged/javafx");

    ProgressBar loadingBar = new ProgressBar(0);
    loadingBar.setMinWidth(400);

    // using binding to easily connect the worker and the progress bar
    loadingBar.progressProperty().bind(
            webEngine.getLoadWorker().progressProperty());

    webEngine.getLoadWorker().stateProperty().addListener(
            (observable, oldValue, newValue) -> {
                if (newValue == Worker.State.SUCCEEDED) {
                    System.out.println("Page was successfully loaded!");
                } else if (newValue == Worker.State.FAILED) {
                    System.out.println("Page loading has failed!");
                }

            });
```

```
VBox root = new VBox(5, loadingBar, webView);
primaryStage.setTitle("JavaFX on SO");
primaryStage.setScene(new Scene(root, 400, 300));
primaryStage.show();
}
```

Here is a screenshot of the application in the middle of loading. Note the progress bar at the top:

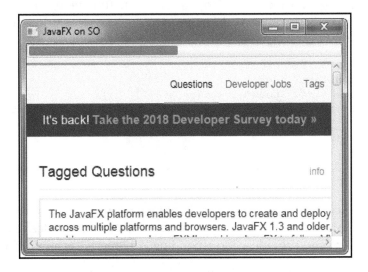

 It's very important to wait for `Worker.State.SUCCEEDED` before starting any work with web page content—both HTML and JavaScript. It's similar to the JavaScript practice of writing code in the `document.onload()` method.

Another way to wait for page loading is the `workDone` property:

```
webEngine.getLoadWorker().workDoneProperty().addListener((observable,
oldValue, newValue) -> {
        if (newValue.intValue() == 100) {
                // page is 100% loaded
        }
});
```

Loading content and user interface callbacks

Besides a particular URL, you can directly provide HTML to WebEngine through the `loadContent()` method:

```
webEngine.loadContent("<input type=button onclick=\"window.alert('hi')\"
value='Click Me!'>");
```

Note that we are calling a JavaScript `window.alert()` method here, which should show an alert window by JavaScript spec. WebEngine can't create new windows by itself, but has a corresponding API we can use:

```
// chapter9/web/WebEngineDemo.java
webEngine.setOnAlert((event) -> {
    Stage stage = new Stage((StageStyle.UTILITY));
    stage.setScene(new Scene(new StackPane(new Label(event.getData())),
100, 80));
    stage.show();
});
webEngine.loadContent("<input type=button onclick=\"window.alert('hi')\"
value='Click Me!'>");
```

A slightly more complex setup is required to handle `window.open()` requests. They are called pop-up requests and you need to create a new `WebView` in the desired location (usually a new `Stage`) and provide a corresponding `WebEngine` as a return value:

```
// chapter9/web/WebEngineDemo.java
webEngine.setCreatePopupHandler((popupFeatures) -> {
    // create a new stage with new webview
    Stage stage = new Stage((StageStyle.UTILITY));
    WebView webViewPopup = new WebView();
    stage.setScene(new Scene(new StackPane(webViewPopup), 300, 300));
    stage.show();
    // return engine from the created webview
    return webViewPopup.getEngine();
});
webEngine.loadContent("<a href='http://www.google.com'>google</a>");
```

Thus the original `WebView` doesn't care how the new window is created (and whether it was created at all); it just asks the provided `WebEngine` to load the corresponding URL:

Here is a list of other supported callbacks; you can find a full list in the WebEngine's JavaDoc:

JavaScript method/property	JavaFX WebEngine callback
`window.confirm()`	`confirmHandler`
`window.open()`/`window.close()` event	`onVisibilityChanged`
`window.prompt()`	`promptHandler`
Setting `window.status`	`onStatusChanged`
Any window resize calls	`onResized`

Note that all these handlers work for `WebEngine.load(URL string)` calls as well. I've used `loadContent()` to show you the corresponding HTML right in the code.

Using Document Object Model

The **Document Object Model (DOM)** can be retrieved through `WebEngine.getDocument()`, which returns an `org.w3c.dom.Document` giving access to the whole web page model.

In the following demonstration, we will find and print all links on a web page using this API:

```
// chapter9/web/DOMModelDemo.java
public void start(Stage stage) {
    WebView webView = new WebView();
    WebEngine webEngine = webView.getEngine();
    webEngine.load("https://stackoverflow.com/questions/tagged/javafx");

    webEngine.getLoadWorker().stateProperty().addListener(
            (observable, oldValue, newValue) -> {
                // remember, we need to get the page loaded first
                if (newValue == Worker.State.SUCCEEDED) {
                    NodeList links =
webEngine.getDocument().getElementsByTagName("a");
                        for (int i = 0; i < links.getLength(); i++) {
                            System.out.println(links.item(i));
                        }
                } else if (newValue == Worker.State.FAILED) {
                    System.out.println("Page loading has failed!");
                }

            });

    stage.setTitle("JavaFX on SO");
    stage.setScene(new Scene(new StackPane(webView), 400, 300));
    stage.show();
}
```

Running JavaScript on a page

You can execute an arbitrary JavaScript by calling `WebEngine.executeScript()`. The return type is not defined; it depends on the type of JavaScript which has been executed, for example, `String`, `Number`, `JSObject`, and so on. You can find a full list in the JavaDoc.

TIP

JavaScript numbers from the same function can be matched to different Java objects on each call—either Double or Integer, depending on JavaScript values. To avoid `instanceof` checks, you can use `java.lang.Number` for all numerical values. See the following example.

In the next example, we will use JavaScript commands to dynamically show an overlay over a `WebView` that will show the bounds of the HTML element under the cursor and its tag name.

For the overlay, we will put a separate transparent pane over the `WebView` and will draw the overlay there. And JavaScript will be used to get the borders and type of the element under the cursor.

For example, we see that the area under the mouse cursor is a **DIV,** as shown in the following screenshot:

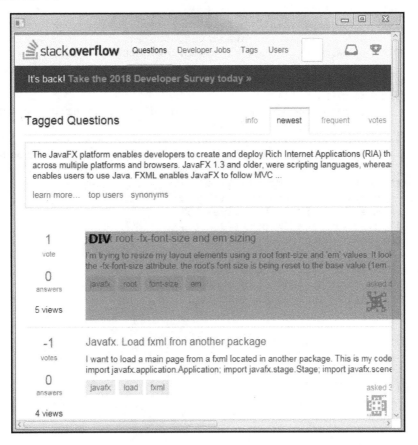

See the inline comments for more details:

```java
// chapter8/web/WebOverlay.java
public void start(Stage stage) {
    WebView webView = new WebView();
    // name of the element shown in the overlay
    Text overlayText = new Text(5, 18, "");
    overlayText.setFont(Font.font(null, FontWeight.BOLD, 20));
    // red overlay
    Pane overlay = new Pane(overlayText);
    overlay.setStyle("-fx-background-color: rgba(255,0,0,0.5);");
    // transparent pane to hold our overlay, it covers all WebView
    Pane pane = new Pane(overlay);
    pane.setPrefSize(600, 600);

    stage.setScene(new Scene(new StackPane(webView, pane), 600, 600));

    pane.setOnMouseMoved((event) -> {
        // calling javascript to find what element is under cursor
        // result is netscape.javascript.JSObject
        JSObject object = (JSObject) webView.getEngine().
            executeScript("document.elementFromPoint(" + event.getX() + ","
+ event.getY() + ");");
        if (object != null) {
            // calculating element's bounds using JavaScript object
            JSObject bounds = (JSObject)
object.call("getBoundingClientRect");
            // converting types from JavaScripts can be ververbose
            overlay.setTranslateX(((Number)
bounds.getMember("left")).doubleValue());
            overlay.setTranslateY(((Number)
bounds.getMember("top")).doubleValue());
            overlay.setMinWidth(((Number)
bounds.getMember("width")).doubleValue());
            overlay.setMinHeight(((Number)
bounds.getMember("height")).doubleValue());
            // finding what this element is
            overlayText.setText((String)object.getMember("tagName"));
        }
    });
    webView.getEngine().load("https://stackoverflow.com/questions/tagged/javafx
");

    stage.show();
}
```

Calling JavaFX code from JavaScript

The user interface callbacks we have talked about were our first example of calling JavaFX code from JavaScript. But you can use such calls not only for preset API methods but also for any logic, for example, as a reaction to a button press.

Let's see how it works.

First of all, you need to get access to the JavaScript `window` object as we already did in the previous section:

```
JSObject window = (JSObject) webEngine.executeScript("window");
```

 Technically, it can be any JavaScript object, not only `window`. We used it for simplicity.

Now you can inject a random object into the `window`:

```
window.setMember("app", this);
```

Given that we call this code in the `start()` method, we are providing a link to the JavaFX application. You can use a specially crafted object instead:

```
MyContext context = new MyContext();
window.setMember("app", context);
```

Now, on the JavaScript side, you have access to the `app` object and can call methods from it. Let's add an extra method to our application:

```
public void test(String param) {
    System.out.println("hi " + param);
}
```

We will load JavaScript to call the preceding method. Note that we can easily pass a parameter to the called method:

```
webEngine.loadContent("<p><input type=button onclick=\"app.test('hi')\"
value='Click Me!'>");
```

I've combined all the pieces together into a more interesting example:

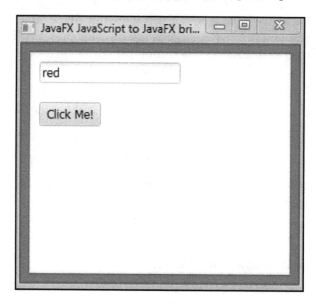

In this example, you can type any color into the HTML textbox and assign it to the JavaFX background of the application; see the details in the inline comments:

```java
// chapter9/web/JS2JavaBridgeDemo.java
public class JS2JavaBridgeDemo extends Application {
    // declaring root as a variable to have access to it from setColor()
method
    StackPane root;

    @Override
    public void start(Stage primaryStage) {
        WebView webView = new WebView();
        WebEngine webEngine = webView.getEngine();

        // here we have an HTML page with a text box and a button
        // pressing the button will take entered text value and
        // pass it to the JavaFX application
        webEngine.loadContent(
                "<p><input type=text id='color' value='red'/>"
            + "<p><input type=button
onclick=\"app.setColor(document.getElementById('color').value)\"
value='Click Me!'>");
        JSObject window = (JSObject) webEngine.executeScript("window");
        window.setMember("app", this);
```

```
        root = new StackPane(webView);
        // adding padding to have visible part of the background
        root.setPadding(new Insets(10));
        primaryStage.setTitle("JavaFX JavaScript to JavaFX bridge demo");
        primaryStage.setScene(new Scene(root, 300, 250));
        primaryStage.show();
    }
    // this method we will be calling from JavaScript
    public void setColor(String param) {
        // taking parameter and apply it as a color to the background
        root.setStyle("-fx-background-color: " + param + ";");
    }

    public static void main(String[] args) {
        launch(args);
    }
}
```

Now you can work with any HTML from JavaFX back and forth. You can enhance existing web pages with JavaFX functionality; provide a similar interface for web access and a JavaFX app for your service; or just use HTML5 capabilities as part of your application.

Incorporating media into a JavaFX application

JavaFX provides the means to play media files in the `javafx.scene.media` package. It supports the following media formats:

- MP3
- MP4
- AIFF
- WAV
- FLV

You can find all the latest details in the JavaDoc: `https://docs.oracle.com/javase/10/docs/api/javafx/scene/media/package-summary.html`.

Adding audio clips

The simplest form of media is an AudioClip, which works best for short sounds such as a button click. Note that AudioClip is not dedicated to longer audio or music sequences for the following reasons:

- It holds the whole clip in memory.
- It doesn't provide any API for choosing the playback time.

The AudioClip API is very simple; it doesn't require any extra objects and is recommended for short sound effects. For longer audio clips, use the Media class described in the next section.

The following formats are supported by the AudioClip class:

- MP3
- AIFF containing uncompressed PCM
- WAV containing uncompressed PCM
- MPEG-4 multimedia container with Advanced Audio Coding (AAC) audio

Here is an example of the button with a click sound:

```
// chapter8/media/AudioClipDemo.java
AudioClip clickSound = new
AudioClip("https://github.com/sgrinev/mastering-javafx-9-10-book/raw/master
/resources/mouse-click.wav");
Button btn = new Button("Hello World");
btn.setOnAction((e) -> {
    clickSound.play();
});
```

 The location of the resource file works the same way as all JavaFX resources we've studied. You can refresh your memory in the *Working with resources* section in Chapter 4, *FXML*.

Working with the MediaPlayer and Media classes

The MediaPlayer class is the class which can play media, either audio or video. It doesn't have any UI controls and for the video playback you need to use the corresponding MediaView class (see the next section).

As you don't need any UI for an audio, let's look at it first. Playing an MP3 song looks as follows:

```
Media media = new Media("http://www.sample-videos.com/audio/mp3/wave.mp3");
MediaPlayer mp = new MediaPlayer(media);
mp.play();
```

You can control playback in various ways using `Media` class properties, APIs, and event handlers; some of them are very similar to `Timeline` ones (see `Chapter 5`, *Animation*). I'll list the most interesting ones:

- `seek (Duration seekTime)`: Sets the playback to the specified time
- `setOnEndOfMedia (Runnable value)`: media end event handler
- `cycleCountProperty`: Repetition count; can be `MediaPlayer.INDEFINITE` for an endless loop
- `volumeProperty`: Controls the media volume, from 0 (silence) to 1.0 (maximal volume)
- `currentTime`: Current media playback time

Another interesting audio API provided by `MediaPlayer` is a spectrum analysis. You can get a list of magnitudes and phases for each frequency. The most obvious use of that data is building an equalizer animation:

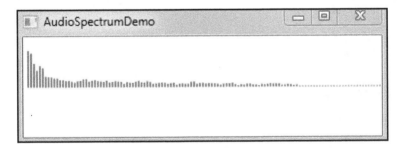

And here is the code; check the comments for the details:

```
// chapter9/media/MediaAudioDemo.java
public void start(Stage primaryStage) {
    final int MID = 50;

    Pane root = new Pane();

    // preparing a line for each frequency
    Line[] lines = new Line[128];
    for (int i = 0; i < 128; i++) {
```

```
        Line line = new Line(5 + i*3, MID, 5 + i*3, MID);
        lines[i] = line;
        root.getChildren().add(line);
    }

    // loading mp3
    Media media = new
Media("https://github.com/sgrinev/mastering-javafx-9-10-book/raw/master/res
ources/808-beat.mp3");
    MediaPlayer mp = new MediaPlayer(media);
    // configuring spectrum listener
    mp.setAudioSpectrumListener(new AudioSpectrumListener() {
        @Override
        public void spectrumDataUpdate(double timestamp, double duration,
float[] magnitudes, float[] phases) {
            for (int i = 0; i < Math.max(128, magnitudes.length); i++) {
                // updating each line according to the corresponding
magnitude value
                lines[i].setEndY(MID - magnitudes[i] +
mp.getAudioSpectrumThreshold());
            }
        }
    });

    primaryStage.setTitle("AudioSpectrumDemo");
    primaryStage.setScene(new Scene(root, 370, 100));
    primaryStage.show();
    mp.play();
}
```

Adding video through MediaView

Finally, for video output, we need `MediaView`:

```
// chapter9/media/MediaVideoDemo.java
public void start(Stage primaryStage) {
    Media media = new
Media("http://www.sample-videos.com/video/mp4/240/big_buck_bunny_240p_1mb.m
p4");
    MediaPlayer mediaPlayer = new MediaPlayer(media);
    MediaView mediaView = new MediaView(mediaPlayer);
```

```
primaryStage.setTitle("VideoSpectrumDemo");
primaryStage.setScene(new Scene(new Pane(mediaView), 320, 240));
primaryStage.show();
mediaPlayer.play();
}
```

Through this short code, we made a small video player on JavaFX:

Having to create three different objects looks excessive, but each level serves a different purpose:

- Media describes the media file: it holds all information such as URL, dimensions (if video), audio tracks, and other info specific to media
- MediaPlayer is a means of running the media: it provides API for controlling playback and retrieving runtime media info such as audio spectrum, and; it also provides handlers for playback events
- MediaView is responsible only for the video representation: it controls only that video location, parameters, and special options such as the viewport

Don't forget that MediaView is just a regular Node on the SceneGraph, so it's capable of all the regular Node functions—you can rotate it, transform it, add any effects, even put it on a 3D space (see Chapter 12, *3D at a Glance*), and it will keep playing.

For example, we can add the `DistortionMap` we used in the previous chapter:

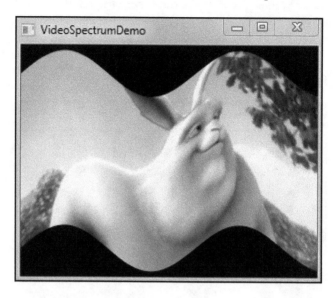

See the following code:

```java
// chapter9/media/MediaVideoEffectsDemo.java
public void start(Stage primaryStage) {
    Media media = new
Media("http://www.sample-videos.com/video/mp4/240/big_buck_bunny_240p_1mb.m
p4");
    MediaPlayer mediaPlayer = new MediaPlayer(media);
    MediaView mediaView = new MediaView(mediaPlayer);

    FloatMap floatMap = new FloatMap();
    floatMap.setWidth(320);
    floatMap.setHeight(240);

    for (int x = 0; x < 320; x++) {
        double v = Math.sin(x / 30.) / 10.;
        for (int y = 0; y < 240; y++) {
            floatMap.setSamples(x, y, 0.0f, (float) v);
        }
    }
```

```
DisplacementMap displacementMap = new DisplacementMap();
displacementMap.setWrap(true);
displacementMap.setMapData(floatMap);
mediaView.setEffect(displacementMap);

primaryStage.setTitle("VideoSpectrumDemo");
primaryStage.setScene(new Scene(new Pane(mediaView), 320, 240));
primaryStage.show();
mediaPlayer.play();
}
```

Summary

In this chapter, we looked at adding audio, video, and web content to a JavaFX application to provide a rich modern interface. In the next chapter, we will learn how to work with complex JavaFX controls, such as tables, charts, and more.

Advanced Controls and Charts

10

Presenting large amounts of data is an important part of modern applications.

In this chapter, we will review JavaFX's capabilities in data presentation, specifically with coverage of the following:

- `ListView`
- `TableView`
- `Charts`

Advanced controls

The most sophisticated JavaFX controls are ones that are dedicated to representing a large amount of data: `ListView` and `TableView`. We will review data management, cell creation, and editable data in the following sections.

ListView

`ListView` is a familiar UI control, which represents a list of items shown in a scrollable column or row:

Despite the simple concept, JavaFX's `ListView` has a large API, providing a lot of options to customize it for your needs.

Managing ListView items

The `ListView` content is backed up by an `ObservableList` and any changes to this list are automatically reflected in the `ListView`, as in the button handler in the next example:

```
// chaptep10/list/ListViewDemo.java
ObservableList<String> items = FXCollections.observableArrayList(
        "Red", "Blue", "Yellow", "Green");
ListView<String> list = new ListView<>(items);

Button btn = new Button("Add New Item");
btn.setOnAction((e) -> {
    items.add(
            // just a way to generate semirandom new items
            items.get(new Random().nextInt(items.size()))
    );
});
```

Using Selection and Focus API

To get the currently selected item, you need to use the `SelectionModel` API:

```
list.getSelectionModel().getSelectedItem();  // item
list.getSelectionModel().getSelectedIndex(); // index
```

It looks a bit wordy, but having all relevant APIs in a helper class is convenient, especially when you want your list to be multi-selectable. To enable multi-select, you need to set `SelectionMode.MULTIPLE`. For example, for the preceding code block it will look as follows:

```
// chaptep10/list/MultiselectDemo.java
list.getSelectionModel().setSelectionMode(SelectionMode.MULTIPLE);
// getting selected items for multi-select
ObservableList<String> selected =
list.getSelectionModel().getSelectedItems();

// tracking selection
list.getSelectionModel().selectedIndexProperty().addListener((obs) -> {
    System.out.println("Selected: "
            list.getSelectionModel().getSelectedItems());
    System.out.println("Focused: " +
            list.getFocusModel().getFocusedItem());
});
```

For multi-selectable lists, one more API becomes important: `FocusModel`. It represents the current item, which can be moved by arrow keys and graphically shown by a rectangle box; see the **Green** element in the next screenshot:

Editable lists

The Cell Factories API provides a flexible way to customize cells in the `ListView` and supports editable lists.

Creating the TextFieldListCell

The simplest cell factory is `TextFieldListCell`. It allows us to double-click on any item in the `ListView` and set a new value, which will be automatically be reflected in the corresponding `ObservableList`. Refer to the following code:

```
// chaptep10/list/TextFieldListCellDemo.java
ObservableList<Integer> items = FXCollections.observableArrayList(
        100, 200, 500, 1000);

ListView<Integer> list = new ListView<>(items);
list.setEditable(true);
list.setCellFactory(TextFieldListCell.forListView(new
                IntegerStringConverter()));

items.addListener(((ListChangeListener.Change<? extends Integer> change) ->
{
    // this will write something like
    // { [500] replaced by [600] at 2 }
    System.out.println(change);
});

stage.setTitle("TextFieldListCell Demo");
stage.setScene(new Scene(new StackPane(list), 200, 200));
stage.show();
```

Now, you can double-click on any field to get an editing UI:

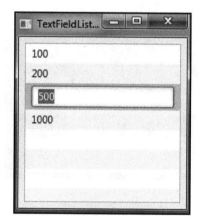

Note that our `ListView` this time holds `Integer`. You don't need to do anything extra to make `ListView` show them; by default, it will use `toString()`. But, to edit values, we need to provide a converter to and from `String`, because `TextField` works with Strings, hence the `IntegerStringConverter` parameter.

> Due to API restrictions, you need to provide a converter even for `String`-based lists. It's called `DefaultStringConverter` and does essentially nothing.

Editing through a ChoiceBox/ComboBox

`ChoiceBox` provides a selection of preset values the user can choose from as a new value for the edited cell.

To use a `ChoiceBox`, we need to have an additional list of the potential new values:

```java
// chaptep10/list/ChoiceBoxListCellDemo.java
ObservableList<String> values = FXCollections.observableArrayList(
        "Red", "Blue", "Yellow", "Green");

ObservableList<String> items = FXCollections.observableArrayList(
        "Gray", "Gray", "Gray", "Gray");

ListView<String> list = new ListView<>(items);
list.setEditable(true);
list.setCellFactory(ChoiceBoxListCell.forListView(values));
```

Note that existing items in the `ListView` are not required to be chosen from `values`:

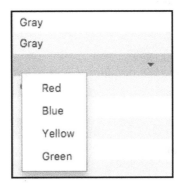

`ComboBoxListCell` works the same way, providing `ComboBox` instead of `ChoiceBox`.

Using CheckBox

This is the most tricky cell factory. It provides a `CheckBox` for each `ListView` item, making it easy to create a todo list-style UI:

For such a list, we can't just use `Strings`, because we need to store the states of the checkboxes. Let's introduce a separate class for that:

```java
private static final class TodoItem {
    final String name;
    final BooleanProperty isDone = new SimpleBooleanProperty(false);

    public TodoItem(String name) {
        this.name = name;
    }

    @Override
    public String toString() {
        return name + (isDone.get() ? " DONE" : "");
    }
}
```

Now, we can use `CheckBoxListCell` by providing a special callback, which will state the corresponding `Boolean` value for each item:

```java
// chaptep10/list/CheckBoxDemo.java
ObservableList<TodoItem> items = FXCollections.observableArrayList(
        new TodoItem("Sign a Contract"), new TodoItem("Fail Deadline"),
        new TodoItem("Blame Yourself"), new TodoItem("Suffer"));
ListView<TodoItem> list = new ListView<>(items);
list.setEditable(true);
list.setCellFactory(CheckBoxListCell.forListView( item -> item.isDone ));
```

The next problem is that our `ObservableList` is based on `TodoItem` elements and has no idea whether something changed inside these objects. So, if you write a similar listener to the one we used previously, it will not work:

```java
// is not called on checkbox click because only TodoItem internal field was
//changed
items.addListener((ListChangeListener.Change<? extends TodoItem> change) ->
{
    // let's print everything here, because default Change output is not
//smart enough
    items.stream().forEach(System.out::println);
});
```

To address that, we need to teach our `ObservableList` about one more layer to track:

```java
ObservableList<TodoItem> items = FXCollections.observableArrayList(
        (TodoItem item) -> new Observable[] { item.isDone });
items.addAll(
        new TodoItem("Sign a Contract"), new TodoItem("Fail Deadline"),
        new TodoItem("Blame Yourself"), new TodoItem("Suffer"));
```

Here, we are using another constructor, which sets the so-called extractor callback: for each `TodoItem`, it adds a new set of `Observable` objects to track. In our case, it's just one value, `item.isDone`.

Note that you can set several `Observables` to watch by the extractor.

And yet, we are still not done. The `TodoItem.toString()` provides too much information to be directly used by `ListView` and will result in the following behavior:

To help with that, we again can provide a `StringConverter`:

```
list.setCellFactory(CheckBoxListCell.forListView(
    item -> item.isDone,
    new StringConverter<TodoItem>() {
        @Override
        public String toString(TodoItem item) {
            return item.name;
        }

        @Override
        public TodoItem fromString(String string) {
            throw new UnsupportedOperationException("We don't need this.");
        }
    }
));
```

Now we have a full-fledged to-do list, which stores its state and looks nice — see the first screenshot in this section.

Creating custom cells

Another role of Cell Factory is creating custom cells for your list with any content, instead of text.

In the following `setCellFactory` method, we will add a color rectangle corresponding to the list-item name:

```
ObservableList<String> items = FXCollections.observableArrayList(
        "Red", "Blue", "Yellow", "Green");
ListView<String> list = new ListView<>(items);

list.setCellFactory((ListView<String> param) -> {
    return new ListCell<>() {
        @Override
        public void updateItem(String item, boolean empty) {
            super.updateItem(item, empty);
            if (! (empty || item == null)) {
                // adding new item
                setGraphic(new Rectangle(30, 30, Color.web(item)));
                setText(item);
            } else {
                setText(null);
                setGraphic(null);
            }
        }
    };
});
```

There are quite a few plumbing code lines here, but the main line is the `setGraphic()` call. It creates an extra graphic element in the list cell:

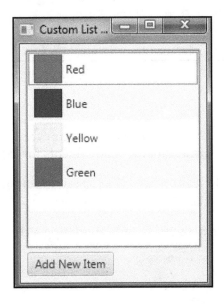

The setGraphic() method is an entry point to the custom ListView (and other controls with a similar API). You can put anything there; for example, the specialized ListCell classes from the previous sections were implemented using this approach.

Using TableView

TableView is an important control, as tables are a very popular and convenient way to present information in the modern UI. Let's see how to work with them in JavaFX:

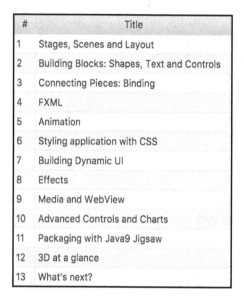

#	Title
1	Stages, Scenes and Layout
2	Building Blocks: Shapes, Text and Controls
3	Connecting Pieces: Binding
4	FXML
5	Animation
6	Styling application with CSS
7	Building Dynamic UI
8	Effects
9	Media and WebView
10	Advanced Controls and Charts
11	Packaging with Java9 Jigsaw
12	3D at a glance
13	What's next?

TableModel

As with a ListView, a TableView is backed up by ObservableList. But, to maintain the model-view connection, there are additional requirements for that list content:

- List elements should be instances of a class, containing table data
- Each element of the class should have a getter

Let's take a look at an example here of a class representing a chapter in this book:

```
// chapter10/table/TableViewDemo.java
class Chapter {
    private final String title;
    private final int number;
```

```java
    public Chapter(int number, String title) {
        this.title = title;
        this.number = number;
    }

    public String getTitle() {
        return title;
    }

    public int getNumber() {
        return number;
    }
}
```

Using this object, we can create a list to be used later as data for a table:

```java
private final ObservableList<Chapter> listChapters
    = FXCollections.observableArrayList(
        new Chapter(1, "Stages, Scenes and Layout"),
        new Chapter(2, "Building Blocks: Shapes, Text and Controls"),
        new Chapter(3, "Connecting Pieces: Binding"),
// ....
```

Creating and combining columns to form tables

Columns in the `TableView` are matched to the field of our `Chapter` class through reflection, so you need to use their fields names as string constants:

```java
TableColumn<Chapter, String> columnTitle = new TableColumn<>("Title");
columnTitle.setCellValueFactory(
            new PropertyValueFactory<>("title"));

TableColumn<Chapter, String> columnNumber = new TableColumn<>("#");
columnNumber.setCellValueFactory(
            new PropertyValueFactory<>("number"));
```

Note we are using `CellValueFactory`, the same concept as in `ListView`, with the same capabilities for further customization.

Now, we can combine all these into a table:

```java
TableView<Chapter> table = new TableView<>();
table.setItems(listChapters);
table.getColumns().add(columnNumber);
table.getColumns().add(columnTitle);
```

`listChapters` is being monitored by `TableView` and any changes in the list will be reflected in the table. You can see it for yourself by adding this code:

```
table.setOnMouseClicked((e)-> {
    listChapters.add(new Chapter(14, "Future chapter"));
});
```

Sorting

`TableView` supports sorting by default; just click on the column headers:

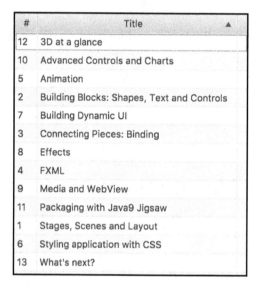

If you want to provide your own sorting logic, you can alter `TableView.comparatorProperty()`.

Observable Model

Previously, our `Chapter` class provided only a minimal set of APIs. The JavaFX documentation advises making all model fields into properties, which allow better flexibility and performance for the `TableView` code.

Let's update our `Chapter` class accordingly:

```java
// chapter10/table/ObservableChapter.java
public class ObservableChapter {

    private final StringProperty titleProp = new SimpleStringProperty();
    private final IntegerProperty numberProp = new SimpleIntegerProperty();

    ObservableChapter(int number, String title) {
        titleProp.set(title);
        numberProp.set(number);
    }

    // Title
    public String getTitle() {
        return titleProp.get();
    }

    public void setTitle(String title) {
        titleProp.set(title);
    }

    public StringProperty titleProperty() {
        return titleProp;
    }

    // Number
    public int getNumber() {
        return numberProp.get();
    }

    public void setNumber(int number) {
        numberProp.set(number);
    }

    public IntegerProperty numberProperty() {
        return numberProp;
    }
}
```

Mind the names; JavaFX uses reflection in `TableView` and all API methods should be conventionally named. In our class, we have these APIs:

- **Getter:** `getFieldname()`
- **Setter:** `setFieldname()`
- **JavaFX property access:** `fieldnameProperty()`

Note the camel case in getter and setter.

Making a table editable

To allow editing of the cell contents, we need to provide two more things, `CellFactory` and `onEditCommit` logic:

```
// chapter10/table/EditableTableViewDemo.java

// TextField based editable cell
columnTitle.setCellFactory(TextFieldTableCell.forTableColumn());
// logic which happes once editing is finished
columnTitle.setOnEditCommit((CellEditEvent<Chapter, String> t) -> {
    // setting new value for the title
    t.getRowValue().setTitle(t.getNewValue());
});

table.setEditable(true);
```

Now, you can double-click on the title cell, enter the new title, and it will be instantly applied to the data model:

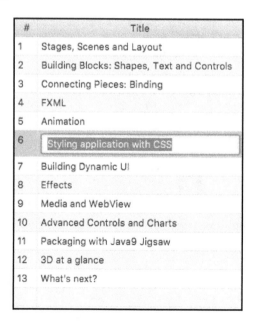

#	Title
1	Stages, Scenes and Layout
2	Building Blocks: Shapes, Text and Controls
3	Connecting Pieces: Binding
4	FXML
5	Animation
6	Styling application with CSS
7	Building Dynamic UI
8	Effects
9	Media and WebView
10	Advanced Controls and Charts
11	Packaging with Java9 Jigsaw
12	3D at a glance
13	What's next?

Working with JavaFX charts

Making charts in JavaFX is easy:

1. Create a list of data in a chart specific format
2. Configure how you want your chart to look

Creating a Pie chart

This chart shows only one dataset as the pie's slices. The bigger a corresponding value, the bigger its slice:

```
// chapter10/chart/PieChartDemo.java
ObservableList<PieChart.Data> pieChartData =
    FXCollections.observableArrayList(
            new PieChart.Data("Luck", 10),
            new PieChart.Data("Skill", 30),
            new PieChart.Data("Power of Will", 15),
            new PieChart.Data("Pleasure", 5),
            new PieChart.Data("Pain", 40));
```

The JavaFX `PieChart` for this looks as follows:

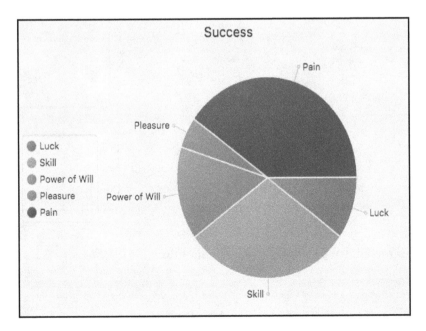

Note that numbers in `PieChart.Data` are not always percents—the total sum is calculated on each new element and each number represents a share of this total sum.

Additionally, all you need to create `PieChart` is to choose the title and legend options:

```
PieChart chart = new PieChart(data);
chart.setTitle("Success");
chart.setLegendSide(Side.LEFT);

stage.setScene(new Scene(chart, 530, 400));
stage.setTitle("Pie Chart Demo");
stage.show();
```

Note that the chart will automatically resize, doing its best to adapt to the new size:

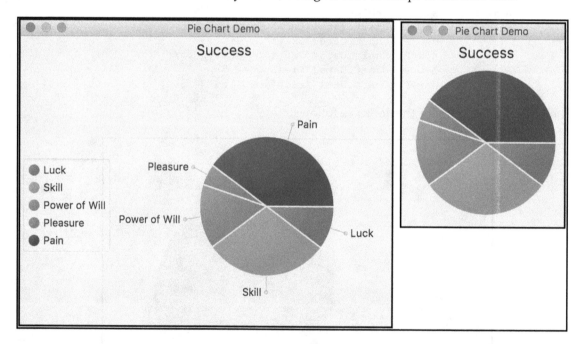

And it can be animated; try this code to see an animation:

```
chart.setOnMouseClicked((e) -> {
    pieChartData.add(new PieChart.Data("Stuff",10));
});
```

The legend is not that useful in our example, so you can either hide it or the chart labels using the `PieChart.setLabelsVisible(boolean value)` and `PieChart.setLegendVisible(boolean value)` methods.

Creating a Line chart

`LineChart` is very similar to a mathematical graph of a function. It requires a few more entities to set up:

- Axes represent vertical and horizontal data
- Series is a set of data shown by one line

For example, in the next screenshot:

- The horizontal axis (or x-axis) represents months of the year
- The vertical axis (or y-axis) shows average temperature in that month
- Each series is a different city's data:

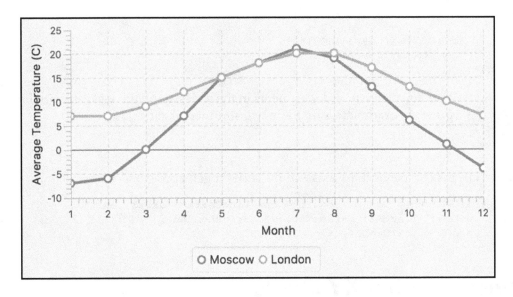

Let's start with the code for axis:

```
// chapter10/chart/LineChartDemo.java

// Months from 1 to 12 with a tick for each one
NumberAxis axisX = new NumberAxis("Month", 1, 12, 1);
// We can skip boundaries and chart will calculate them automatically!
NumberAxis axisY = new NumberAxis();
axisY.setLabel("Average Temperature (C)");
```

Here, we are using numbers on both axes. If you want more complex axis data, you can use `CategoryAxis` and `LineChart<String, Number>` instead.

The next step is the `XYChart.Series` API. You need to choose a name and provide a list of data points on the graph:

```
XYChart.Series<Number, Number> seriesMoscow = new XYChart.Series<>(
    "Moscow", // name
    FXCollections.observableArrayList( // data
        new XYChart.Data<>(1, -7),
        new XYChart.Data<>(2, -6),
        new XYChart.Data<>(3, 0),
        // ...
        new XYChart.Data<>(11, 1),
        new XYChart.Data<>(12, -4)
));
```

You don't have to order elements in the series along the x-axis like in the previous example. `LineChart` will sort them itself.

Now, we just need to connect the axis and the series together to get a chart:

```
LineChart<Number, Number> chart = new LineChart<>(axisX, axisY);
chart.getData().addAll(seriesMoscow, seriesLondon);
Scene scene = new Scene(chart, 500, 350);
```

Review of other XY charts

The rest of the charts are just variations of a line chart. You can use the same code to show most of them, like in the next screenshot:

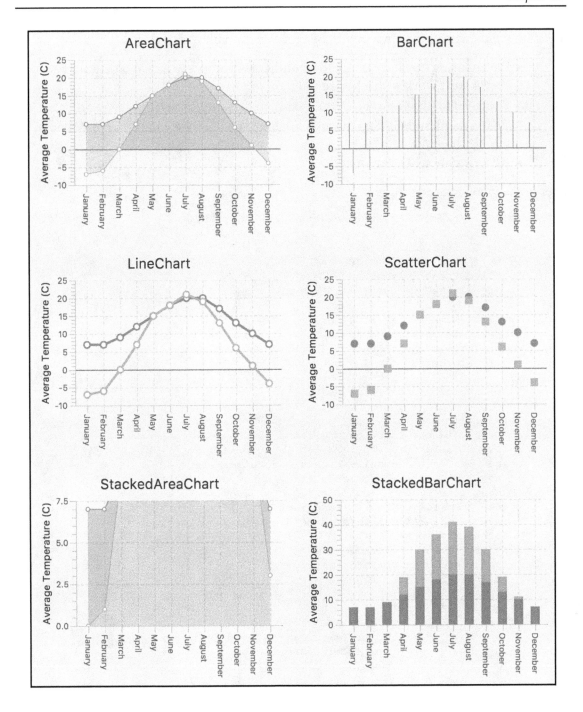

There are these interesting points in the code for this example:

- We are using `CategoryAxis` for months to show a new API and because bar charts don't work with a horizontal `NumberAxis`
- You need to provide a separate instance of axes and series for each chart
- Charts monitor their data through binding, so to add new data you just need to update the series lists
- All new data will be animated

Refer to the following code snippet:

```java
// chapter10/chart/XYChartsDemo.java

public void start(Stage stage) {
    // we need a bit of lambdacraft to work with constructors
    Supplier<CategoryAxis> supplierX = () -> {
        return new CategoryAxis();
    };
    Supplier<NumberAxis> supplierY = () -> {
        NumberAxis axisY = new NumberAxis();
        axisY.setLabel("Average Temperature (C)");
        return axisY;
    };
    TilePane root = new TilePane(2, 2);

    Stream.of(
        // API is the same, only class name changes:
        new AreaChart<>(supplierX.get(), supplierY.get()),
        new BarChart<>(supplierX.get(), supplierY.get()),
        new LineChart<>(supplierX.get(), supplierY.get()),
        new ScatterChart<>(supplierX.get(), supplierY.get()),
        new StackedAreaChart<>(supplierX.get(), supplierY.get()),
        new StackedBarChart<>(supplierX.get(), supplierY.get())
    ).forEach((chart)-> {
        chart.setTitle(chart.getClass().getSimpleName());
        chart.setLegendVisible(false);
        chart.setPrefSize(350, 280);
        XYChart.Series<String, Number> seriesMoscow = new XYChart.Series<>(
                "Moscow",
                FXCollections.observableArrayList(
                        new XYChart.Data<>("January", -7),
                        new XYChart.Data<>("February", -6),
                        new XYChart.Data<>("March", 0),
                        new XYChart.Data<>("April", 7),
                        new XYChart.Data<>("May", 15),
                        new XYChart.Data<>("June", 18),
```

```
                    new XYChart.Data<>("July", 21),
                    new XYChart.Data<>("August", 19),
                    new XYChart.Data<>("September", 13),
                    new XYChart.Data<>("October", 6),
                    new XYChart.Data<>("November", 1),
                    new XYChart.Data<>("December", -4)
            ));

    XYChart.Series<String, Number> seriesLondon = new XYChart.Series<>(
            "London",
            FXCollections.observableArrayList(
                    new XYChart.Data<>("January", 7),
                    new XYChart.Data<>("February", 7),
                    new XYChart.Data<>("March", 9),
                    new XYChart.Data<>("April", 12),
                    new XYChart.Data<>("May", 15),
                    new XYChart.Data<>("June", 18),
                    new XYChart.Data<>("July", 20),
                    new XYChart.Data<>("August", 20),
                    new XYChart.Data<>("September", 17),
                    new XYChart.Data<>("October", 13),
                    new XYChart.Data<>("November", 10),
                    new XYChart.Data<>("December", 7)
            ));
    chart.getData().addAll(seriesLondon, seriesMoscow);
    chart.setOnMouseClicked((e) -> {
        // animated update demo
        seriesMoscow.getData().add(
            new XYChart.Data<>("Nonexistembr", Math.random()*15));
    });
    root.getChildren().add(chart);
});
stage.setScene(new Scene(root, 720, 600));
stage.show();
}
```

Custom controls

In this section, we will look at how to create your own controls and provide different skins for them.

Skins

In JavaFX, controls were created with the Model-View-Controller pattern in mind. The `Control` class itself is responsible for the Model/Controller part—it holds data, state, and logic to work with those. Each control has a corresponding `Skin` class which is responsible for the view—the visual representation of the control.

 There is also a `BehaviorBase` class that provides an option to split the Model and Controller of the `Control`, but unfortunately, it's an internal API. Maybe, JavaFX developers will make it public in future releases.

ClockControl demo

Let's see how skins work using our `ClockControl` demo. We will create two different skins for it and will provide an option to switch between them.

Our skins will be called Hands and Text—let's start with the control that will manage them and other `ClockControl` logic. Note the next points:

- As we are making a proper control now, we can extend the `javafx.scene.control.Control` itself.
- This implements the `Skinnable` interface to work with skins.
- As a Model, our `ClockControl` holds the data—the current time in the `timeProp` field.
- As a Controller, our `ClockControl` handles the *business logic*—updating the `timeProp` field.
- We have a good MVC separation now—our skins will not know how `timeProp` is managed. So, if you decide to move it backward or add *pause* functionality, it can be managed from the `ClockControl` class only.

Refer to the following code snippet:

```java
// chapter10/skins/ClockControl.java
public class ClockControl extends Control {
    // enum to select between our skin types
    public enum SkinType { HANDS, TEXT };
    private final SkinType skinType;

    // implementing a method from Skinnable interface
    @Override
```

```
protected Skin<?> createDefaultSkin() {
    if (skinType == SkinType.HANDS)
        return new ClockSkinHands(this);
    else
        return new ClockSkinText(this);
}

// this is our model data — timeProp
final ObjectProperty<Date> timeProp = new SimpleObjectProperty<>(new
Date());
public ObjectProperty<Date> timeProperty() {
    return timeProp;
}
public ClockControl(SkinType skinType) {
    this.skinType = skinType;
    // this is out "business logic" — updating time value
    Timeline ttimer = new Timeline(new KeyFrame(Duration.seconds(1),
            (event) -> {
                timeProp.setValue(new Date());
            }));
    ttimer.setCycleCount(Timeline.INDEFINITE);
    ttimer.playFrom(Duration.millis(999));
}
}
```

Now, let's see create our skins starting from the easier one—ClockSkinText. All skins are aware of their control types and must implement, Skin<Control> interface. In our case, it will be Skin<ClockControl>.

In the Skin, we need to follow the next four steps:

- Create all UI elements of the skin
- Implement the getSkinnable() method, which returns the control we are *skinning*
- Implement the getNode() method, which returns the root of our skin's SceneGraph
- Omplement (or keep empty) method dispose() where cleanup logic can be

Refer to the following code snippet:

```
// chapter10/skins/ClockSkinText.java
public class ClockSkinText implements Skin<ClockControl> {

    private final ClockControl control;
    private final StackPane root;
```

```java
    private final Text txtTime = new Text();

    // skin creation
    public ClockSkinText(ClockControl control) {
        this.control = control;
        Rectangle border = new Rectangle(120, 50, Color.TRANSPARENT);
        border.setStroke(Color.BLACK);
        root = new StackPane(txtTime, border);
        txtTime.setFont(FONT);
        // connecting text clock with our model value
        txtTime.textProperty().bind(
                Bindings.createStringBinding(() -> {
                    Date date = control.timeProp.get();
                    return date == null ? "" : FORMAT.format(date);
                }, control.timeProp)
        );
    }

    // this Skin method returns the control we are "skinning"
    @Override
    public ClockControl getSkinnable() {
        return control;
    }

    // this Skin method returns root node of our skin
    @Override
    public Node getNode() {
        return root;
    }

    // this method can be used to clean any used resources
    @Override
    public void dispose() {
        // we have nothing to clean up
    }

    // constants
    private static final Font FONT = Font.font ("Courier New",
FontWeight.BOLD, FontPosture.REGULAR, 20);
    private static final SimpleDateFormat FORMAT = new
SimpleDateFormat("hh:mm:ss");
}
```

Our test skin will look like this:

```
03:42:19
```

The `ClockSkinHands` class looks very familiar to the one from Chapter 6, *Styling Applications with CSS*. Only here the `Skin` interface plumbing was added and all logic was moved to the `ClockControl` class:

```
// chapter10/skins/ClockSkinHands.java
public class ClockSkinHands implements Skin<ClockControl> {

    private final ClockControl control;
    private final Pane root;
    private final Rotate rotateSecondHand = new Rotate(0, 0, 0);
    private final Rotate rotateMinuteHand = new Rotate(0, 0, 0);
    private final Rotate rotateHourHand = new Rotate(0, 0, 0);
    public ClockSkinHands(ClockControl control) {
        this.control = control;
        // create minutes hand
        Path minuteHand = new Path(
                new MoveTo(0, 0),
                new LineTo(15, -5),
                new LineTo(100, 0),
                new LineTo(15, 5),
                new ClosePath());
        minuteHand.setFill(Color.DARKGRAY);
        minuteHand.getTransforms().add(rotateMinuteHand);
        minuteHand.setTranslateX(minuteHand.getBoundsInLocal().getWidth() /
2);

        // create second hand
        Line secondHand = new Line(0, 0, 90, 0);
        secondHand.getTransforms().add(rotateSecondHand);
        secondHand.setTranslateX(secondHand.getBoundsInLocal().getWidth() /
2);

        // create hour hand
        Shape hourHand = new Path(
                new MoveTo(0, 0),
                new LineTo(20, -8),
                new LineTo(60, 0),
                new LineTo(20, 8),
                new ClosePath());
```

```
        hourHand.setFill(Color.LIGHTGRAY);
        hourHand.getTransforms().add(rotateHourHand);
        hourHand.setTranslateX(hourHand.getBoundsInLocal().getWidth() / 2);

        root = new StackPane(minuteHand, hourHand, secondHand);
        root.setMinSize(200, 200);
        // binding hands to the model value
        control.timeProperty().addListener((e, oldValue, newValue) -> {
                rotateSecondHand.setAngle(newValue.getSeconds() * 6 -
90);
                rotateMinuteHand.setAngle(newValue.getMinutes() * 6 -
90);
                rotateHourHand.setAngle(newValue.getHours() * 30 - 90);
            });
    }

    @Override
    public ClockControl getSkinnable() {
        return control;
    }

    @Override
    public Node getNode() {
        return root;
    }

    @Override
    public void dispose() {
    }
}
```

Now, let's create a demo that will show both skins together:

```
// chapter10/skins/ClockDemo.java
public void start(Stage stage) {
    Scene scene = new Scene(new HBox(50,
            new ClockControl(ClockControl.SkinType.HANDS),
            new ClockControl(ClockControl.SkinType.TEXT)
    ), 400, 250);
    stage.setScene(scene);
    stage.setTitle("Clock, chapter 10");

    stage.show();
}
```

See the resulting screenshot:

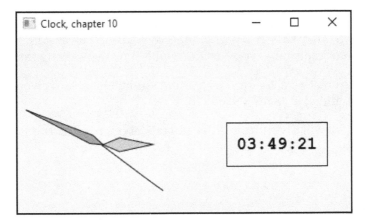

Java 9 and 10 API for skins

Besides creating controls from scratch, you can skin existing controls. Before Java9, you would have to refer to an internal API, which is unreliable, and not possible in modular applications.

In Java9, all controls skins were moved to the public API and heavily reworked to minimize the use of other internal APIs. This allows for extending them and modifying to meet your needs.

However, note that creating a skin for JavaFX controls is a complex task and is required only if you need the control to look completely different. Like two skins in our `ClockControl` example above. For all other cases, there is usually enough customizing options in CSS and Control's API.

Also, studying these skins is a good way to understand how controls work under the hood.

You can find new API classes in the `javafx.scene.control.skin` package.

Summary

In this chapter, we covered charts, tables, and lists, and addressed the most common questions about them. They're only a part of the Advanced Controls API, but after mastering the main concepts here, you can work with the others pretty intuitively.

Also, we looked into creating a custom control and studied how skins work in JavaFX, and which new API was added in JavaFX 9 and 10.

In the next chapter, we will divert from APIs and talk about preparing a JavaFX application for end-user delivery.

11
Packaging with Java9 Jigsaw

When we become handy with JavaFX features, we usually start thinking about presenting their application to customers or peers.

To address that, we will cover the following topics in this chapter:

- Preparing JavaFX applications for end users
- Making executable JavaFX binaries that don't depend on Java Runtime
- New packaging options provided by the Java9 Jigsaw feature

Handmaking JAR files

The default Java application delivery mechanism is JAR files, which are ZIP archives with some extra information that makes them executable by Java. You can store class files (compiled Java files) and resources together in the JAR file.

Most of the IDEs you use will create a JAR file from your project, but in this section, we will review how it works *under the hood*.

Besides the direct download, there are also Java Web Start and browser plugin options, but they are being deprecated by Oracle so I'll leave them out of this book's scope.

Running the demo project

Let's consider the next project structure for the following examples:

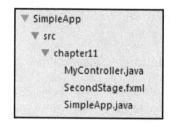

I won't print all the source code here as the exact content is not important for the topic. It's an application that opens the second window loaded from FXML. As always, the source code can be found in the `Chapter11` folder on our GitHub.

Before we package anything, we need to compile our files by calling `javac`. The following CLI commands will compile everything for us:

```
cd SimpleApp
javac -d build/classes src/chapterEleven/*.java
cp src/chapterEleven/SecondStage.fxml build/classes/chapterEleven/
```

Here, we ask `javac` to build all the Java files in our `source` folder and put them into the `build/classes` folder. Note, on line 3, that we need to copy all non-Java files, such as FXML, manually, as `javac` doesn't understand them. If you are on Windows and don't use any Linux mimicking tools, such as Cygwin or MinGW, your line 3 will look like this:

```
copy src\chapterEleven\SecondStage.fxml build\classes\chapterEleven
```

Now, our project's directory structure will appear as shown in the following screenshot:

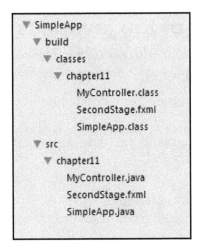

For convenience, I've chosen folder names similar to NetBeans' built project structure. Thus you can look into our other projects and easily recognize the layout.

Now, we can run our application directly:

```
java -cp build/classes/ chapterEleven.SimpleApp
```

Here is an example of both windows and FXML loaded properly:

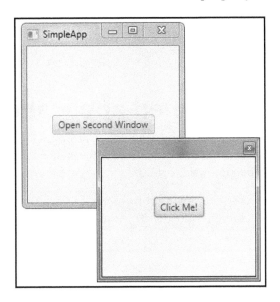

In the next section, we'll create the JAR files for this project.

Basic commands of the javapackager tool

Since Java 8, there is a tool that helps with packaging, named `javapackager`. It has many options but here we are looking only for the `-createjar` command:

You need to set quite a few parameters:

```
"$JAVA_HOME/bin/javapackager" -createjar -appclass chapterEleven.SimpleApp
-outdir dist -outfile SimpleApp.jar -srcdir build/classes
```

Let's review them one by one:

- `"$JAVA_HOME/bin/javapackager"`: `javapackager` is located in the same folder as Java; I have placed parenthesis here to avoid issues with a space in my Windows path
- `-appclass chapterEleven.SimpleApp`: This is the full name of the main class of our application
- `-outdir dist`: The name of the folder for the resulting JAR
- `-outfile SimpleApp.jar`: The name of the JAR
- `-srcdir build/classes`: All class file's resources; `javapackager` will take all the files from this folder and put them into into the JAR, keeping the directory structure

Now, we have a JAR that we can run:

```
java -jar dist/SimpleApp.jar
```

Creating self-contained applications

Distributing JAR files has one major inconvenience—it requires Java runtime (JRE) on the user's computer. And, if you want to use the latest features or rely on certain bugfixes, the version of this runtime also becomes important.

For mature commercial level projects, the requirements are usually stated on the download page, or their installer scripts are enhanced with runtime checks on the client side.

But, if you want to simplify your app to the users, there is an option to distribute a Java runtime alongside an application (or a Self-Contained Application). However, note the following cons to this approach:

- You'll lose the *run anywhere* feature and will have to prepare a separate installer for each platform (such as Windows, masOS, or Linux)
- You need an actual OS installation to create a corresponding bundle
- The runtime is relatively large, so the final binary will grow in size (but we'll look into addressing that in the next section)

Creating Linux images is pretty easy using docker (www.docker.com), which can be run on almost any other platforms; for Windows, image cloud services can be used (such as AWS or Azure) with free tires, but for Mac you need an actual macOS machine or one of the *rent mac in cloud* services.

Preparing OS-native installers with javapackager

Once we have a JAR, we can create a self-containing application using the −deploy command with the −native parameter:

```
"$JAVA_HOME/bin/javapackager" -deploy -native -verbose -appclass
chapterEleven.SimpleApp
-outdir dist-native  -outfile SimpleApp
-srcdir dist -srcfiles SimpleApp.jar
-appclass chapterEleven.SimpleApp -name SimpleApp
```

Parameters are similar to the JAR creation routine, but we need to provide a JAR here as a source.

javapackager may ask you to install additional software to run properly. For example, on Windows you'll need to have the following applications:

- **WiX Toolset** (http://wixtoolset.org/): Windows installer's tools
- **Inno Setup** (http://www.jrsoftware.org): Another installer's toolkit used to generate a .exe installer

This command will populate a dist-native folder with native executables (for example, .exe and .msi on windows) and Java runtime as a dependency for it:

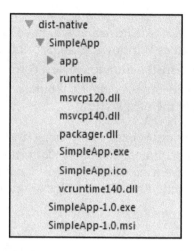

If you run SimpleApp.exe from the SimpleApp folder, you'll directly run a JavaFX application even on a machine without Java installed.

The SimpleApp-1.0.exe and SimpleApp-1.0.msi files are installers that can set up a similar SimpleApp folder on any machine.

On Windows, the size of the resulting folder is 180 Mb. It seems too much for a 3 Kb JAR—but Java9 Jigsaw can help with this, as we will see in the next section.

Working with Jigsaw modules

One of the most prominent features of Java9 was the long-awaited modularization. This feature, called Jigsaw, split a monolithic Java into separate modules. They can be used to create a custom subset of JRE, as is required by specific applications, and impose better rules on the visibility of Java packages/modules.

There are about 80 modules in Java10. Here is the list of modules related to JavaFX:

- javafx.base: Basic JavaFX elements: Properties, bindings, collections, and events
- javafx.graphics: Visual elements: Scenegraph API, shapes, colors, effects, animations, CSS, and so on

- `javafx.controls`: All JavaFX Controls and corresponding APIs
- `javafx.fxml`: FXML API
- `javafx.media`: Video and audio content support
- `javafx.swing`: API to intermix Swing and JavaFX components
- `javafx.web`: WebView component

For almost every JavaFX application, you'll first need two modules; `javafx.base` and `javafx.graphics`. The rest depends on the specific APIs you are using.

Let's see how it might help us with our SimpleApp project.

Making our own module

To make most of the modularization, we should start with creating our own module:

1. First, let's see which modules are used in our small applications using the `jdeps` tool:

   "$JAVA_HOME/bin/jdeps" --generate-module-info . dist/SimpleApp.jar

   This call will generate a `module-info.java` file that describes our application as a module:

   ```
   module chapterEleven {
       requires javafx.base;
       requires javafx.controls;

       requires transitive javafx.fxml;
       requires transitive javafx.graphics;

       exports chapterEleven;
   }
   ```

   We see that our application depends on only four modules (and `java.base`, which is always included).

2. Unfortunately, `jdeps` missed one more thing, which we need to add manually:

```
opens chapterEleven to javafx.fxml;
```

This line is required in the `module-info.java` to allow FXML to work. FXML uses a lot of reflection calls to map XML tags to real JavaFX objects and requires special access rights. By adding this line, you give JavaFX FXML code access to your project's classes' private fields.

3. For the next step, we will recompile our project to make it modular:

```
javac -d build/classes src/chapterEleven/*.java src/module-
info.java
cp src/chapterEleven/SecondStage.fxml build/classes/chapterEleven/
```

4. Now we can prepare a minimal **Java Runtime Environment** (**JRE**) that is capable of running our application using the `jlink` command (it should be one line but I split it a bit to improve readability):

```
jlink --module-path "dist;$JAVA_HOME/jmods" --add-modules
chapterEleven --output dist-10
--strip-debug --compress 2 --no-header-files --no-man-pages
--launcher chapterEleven=chapterEleven/chapterEleven.SimpleApp
```

Here, we specify the folder with our module and base Java modules by the `--module-path` command, set several compression options, and the last parameter is our main class to start an application.

In the output folder, `dist-10`, we will get minimal JRE with our application installed.

5. We can try it now by using the following:

```
dist-10/bin/chapterEleven.bat
```

And, the size of the resulting folder is four times less than the full JRE we received in the previous section.

For your convenience, I've collected all the commands into the following file from the book's GitHub:

```
Chapter11/SimpleApp/build.sh
```

Summary

In this chapter, we stepped out from writing code and reviewed the creation of the deliverables that can be provided to other users. We also learned about the modularization provided by Java9 and 10 , studied JavaFX from the module's point of view, and used new Java9 tools to provide a smaller Java Runtime-independent deliverable.

In the next chapter, we'll learn the basics of writing 3D applications with JavaFX.

12
3D at a Glance

3D is a great way of displaying real-life objects or their models. It's used in a lot of applications nowadays, from action games to educational programs.

In this chapter, we'll go through building a few small 3D applications using the JavaFX 3D API, covering the following topics:

- 3D elements
- Camera
- Light
- Materials

Introduction to the JavaFX 3D API

3D programming is a huge topic that is way beyond the scope of this book. Also the capabilities of JavaFX 3D are limited, so I'll only introduce you to several basic elements and concepts to create some cool examples.

Basic 3D elements

JavaFX works with 3D elements using the same Scene concept, but adds a third dimension in the form of a Z-coordinate. JavaFX provides a few basic 3D shapes (`javafx.scene.shape.Shape3D`) to start with:

- Box
- Cylinder
- Sphere

For more complex figures, there is a class, `MeshView`, that can be used to hold a polygon mesh.

A polygon mesh is a collection of vertices, edges, and faces that defines the shape of a polyhedral object in 3D computer graphics and solid modeling.

Unfortunately, there is no built-in way to import meshes made in 3D modeling tools like Maya, but there is a free open source tool that converts 3D model formats into JavaFX meshes, `http://www.interactivemesh.org/models/jfx3dimporter.html`.

Adding Camera to the Scene

To present a 3D scene to a user we need to specify where this user is located in the virtual 3D space of an application. The corresponding API class is called `javafx.scene.Camera`. Let's see how to create a simple Scene with `PerspectiveCamera` and a 3D element:

Refer to the following code snippet:

```
// chapter12/Basic3dDemo.java
public void start(Stage stage) {
    // creating a 3D cylinder
    Cylinder cylinder = new Cylinder(40, 120);
    cylinder.setRotationAxis(new Point3D(50, 50, 0));
    cylinder.setRotate(45);
```

```
cylinder.setTranslateX(150);
cylinder.setTranslateY(150);
cylinder.setTranslateZ(600);

// setting up camera
PerspectiveCamera camera = new PerspectiveCamera(false);
camera.setTranslateX(100);
camera.setTranslateY(0);
camera.setTranslateZ(300);

// adding camera and cylinder to the scene
Group root = new Group(cylinder);
Scene scene = new Scene(root, 300, 300, true);
scene.setCamera(camera);

stage.setScene(scene);
stage.setTitle("3D shapes demo");
stage.show();

}
```

Let's also add a way to change the camera's location by moving the mouse to better see the three-dimensionality of the scene:

```
scene.setOnMouseMoved((event) -> {
        camera.setTranslateX(event.getSceneX()-50);
        camera.setTranslateY(event.getSceneY()-200);
        camera.setTranslateZ( 300 - event.getSceneX()/2 );
    });
```

With this code, you can rotate the scene and see our shape from different angles:

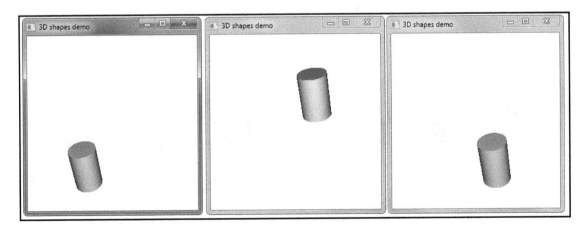

Lighting the Scene

The next important element of the 3D scene is a light source.

There are two types of light:

- `PointLight`, which works like a lamp
- `AmbientLight`, which softly lights from all directions

You can use `AmbientLight` to subtly adjust the coloring of the scene. `PointLight` plays the more important role of an actual light source. Let's add `PointLight` to our example, and make it follow the mouse cursor instead of the camera:

```
// chapter12/LightDemo.java

PointLight light = new PointLight();
light.setTranslateX(350);
light.setTranslateY(100);
light.setTranslateZ(300);

scene.setOnMouseMoved((event) -> {
    light.setTranslateX(event.getSceneX()-50);
    light.setTranslateY(event.getSceneY()-200);
    light.setTranslateZ( 300 - event.getSceneX()/2 );
});

// note you need to add light directly to the scene
Group root = new Group(cylinder, cylinder2, light);
```

Here are some screenshots of our scene with the different positions of the light source:

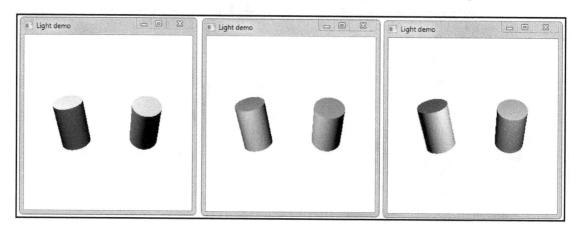

I've added the second cylinder for comparison and better visibility to understand the light's location.

 The light for the 3D scene is a different API from the Effects light that we talked about in Chapter 8, *Effects*. They look similar, but the latter one only *imitates* the light to provide a pseudo-3D effect.

Using Materials

Materials is a way to describe the surface of your 3D objects and how they interact with light. To work with Material's you need to create an instance of the `PhongMaterial` class and use one of its properties.

Let's review how we can enhance a 3D object's surface with different materials.

Using Bump Map

Bump Map uses colors in the image to imitate small displacement on the surface of a 3D object. It's a great way to add small texture details to 3D objects. It saves you the great effort of describing them in 3D terminology.

For example, take a look at the next bump map image and the 3D object affected by it:

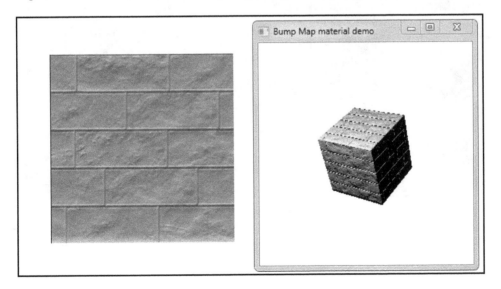

To achieve that, you need to call `material.setBumpMap(Image bumpImage)`:

```
PhongMaterial material= new PhongMaterial();
material.setBumpMap(new Image(
"https://upload.wikimedia.org/wikipedia/commons/8/86/IntP_Brick_NormalMap.p
ng"));

Box box = new Box(100, 100, 100);
box.setTranslateX(250);
box.setTranslateY(100);
box.setTranslateZ(400);
box.setRotate(50);
box.setRotationAxis(new Point3D(100, 100, 0));
box.setMaterial(material);
```

Working with the Diffuse and Self-Illumination maps

These maps work with color, attaching a provided image, such as a wallpaper, to the surface of a 3D object. `SelfIlluminationMap` also adds an additional inside glow to the image.

For example, let's take a map of Earth and put it on a sphere:

It will look as shown in the following screenshots. Note that I've added a rotation to make the results more visible:

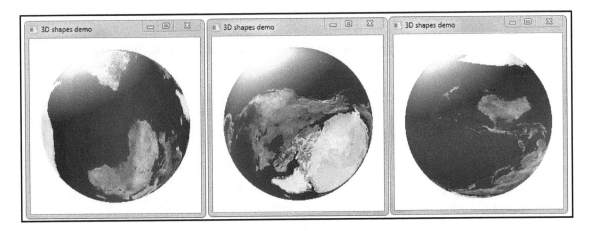

The material method I've used here is `material.setSelfIlluminationMap(Image bumpImage)`. See the inline comments for more details:

```
// chapter12/EarthDemo.java
public void start(Stage stage) {
    // preparing a material
    PhongMaterial mat = new PhongMaterial();
    Image image = new Image(
"https://upload.wikimedia.org/wikipedia/commons/thumb/e/ed/Reversed_Earth_m
ap_1000x500.jpg/800px-Reversed_Earth_map_1000x500.jpg");
    // we took an Earth map and used it as a material
    mat.setSelfIlluminationMap(image);

    // creating sphere
    Sphere sphere = new Sphere(150);
    sphere.setTranslateX(450);
    sphere.setTranslateY(300);
    sphere.setTranslateZ(400);
    sphere.setRotationAxis(new Point3D(1, 1, 0));
    // attaching our map material to the sphere
    sphere.setMaterial(mat);

    // adding a point light at the top of the scene
    PointLight light = new PointLight(Color.LIGHTYELLOW);
    light.setTranslateX(350);
    light.setTranslateY(100);
    light.setTranslateZ(300);

    // setting the camera
    PerspectiveCamera camera = new PerspectiveCamera(false);
    camera.setTranslateX(300);
    camera.setTranslateY(150);
```

```
    camera.setTranslateZ(300);

    Scene scene = new Scene(new Group(sphere, light), 300, 300, true);
    scene.setCamera(camera);
    stage.setScene(scene);
    stage.setTitle("3D shapes demo");
    stage.show();

    // this animation will rotate a sphere for us, so viewer can see a
whole globe
    RotateTransition rot = new RotateTransition(Duration.seconds(10),
sphere);
    rot.setToAngle(360);
    rot.setInterpolator(Interpolator.LINEAR);
    rot.setCycleCount(Timeline.INDEFINITE);
    rot.play();
}
```

Note how, at the end of the sample, we used an Animation API—it works with 3D objects in the same way as with 2D ones.

Summary

In this chapter, we briefly looked at the JavaFX 3D API and learned some basic 3D concepts; camera, light, and materials. The JavaFX 3D API is not very developed yet, but it allows users to build moderately complex 3D demos and games that work with acceptable performance, and can utilize users' graphics cards.

We reviewed two important approaches to presenting 3D scenes to the viewer; moving the camera and using an animation.

This was our last chapter about the API. In the next chapter, I'll describe other resources and topics you may use in the further mastering of JavaFX.

13
What's Next?

Congratulations—you've got through the whole book! But, that doesn't mean that your JavaFX journey has to end. There is a lot of other information about JavaFX, both from its creators and from enthusiasts. In this chapter, we will review:

- Various sites where you can study JavaFX
- JavaFX frameworks and libraries
- Blogs
- JavaFX's future

Other materials

For further information about JavaFX, you can refer to the following sources.

Official documentation of JavaFX

JavaFX JavaDoc is a very good source for any extra information you want to know about the JavaFX API. It's usually accompanied with examples, and can be quite thorough.

JavaDoc can be found online: `https://docs.oracle.com/javase/10/docs/api/overview-summary.html`. Also, it's included in the JDK distribution and most IDEs will show it in code completion, or by a shortcut.

Besides JavaDoc, there are great reference guides to FXML and CSS in the official documentation:

- **FXML:** `https://docs.oracle.com/javase/10/docs/api/javafx/fxml/doc-files/introduction_to_fxml.html`
- **CSS:** `https://docs.oracle.com/javase/10/docs/api/javafx/scene/doc-files/cssref.html`

The JavaFX articles set, unfortunately, hasn't been updated much since Java8, but still, it is a good source of information, https://docs.oracle.com/javase/8/javase-clienttechnologies.htm.

Stackoverflow.com

If you are not yet familiar with stackoverflow.com, you should try it immediately. It's the greatest Q&A site about programming (and other stuff on its network's domains).

There are over 20,000 questions answered about JavaFX already. And, if you don't find your specific question, you can always ask a new one. JavaFX tags are monitored by several experienced users, and questions are usually answered within a few hours.

The main StackOverflow address for JavaFX is https://stackoverflow.com/tags/javafx.

Working with JavaFX source code

Don't forget that JavaFX is open source and you can just go and check any API code to see how it works.

You can either download it from http://hg.openjdk.java.net/jdk/jdk10 or, again, use Java IDEs, which usually allow viewing a Java source by clicking on the name of the method or class you are interested in.

Beyond the official API

JavaFX is not just the API you get from the installation. There is a large range of libraries, frameworks, and technologies created by third-party developers.

There is a great list of such items at https://github.com/mhrimaz/AwesomeJavaFX. There are dozens of entries there, so I'll list the ones I consider to be the most interesting next.

Frameworks and libraries

- **ControlsFX** (http://fxexperience.com/controlsfx/) provides a great range of controls, from advanced ones such as SpreadsheetView to small but convenient ones such as Borders.

- **JFXtras** (`http://jfxtras.org/`) is a huge JavaFX extension library with utility classes, new controls, and various enhancements.
- **TestFX** (`https://github.com/TestFX/TestFX`) is a simple and convenient test framework.
- **JxBrowser** (`https://jxbrowser.support.teamdev.com/support/home`) is an alternative to JavaFX WebView, based on Chromium and supporting a wider set of browser functionality. It doesn't use the JavaFX graphics engine, but can be used in any JavaFX application.
- **EasyBind** (`https://github.com/TomasMikula/EasyBind`) takes binding to another level, greatly simplifying and enhancing JavaFX binding functionality.

Blogs

Several former JavaFX developers and enthusiasts are writing a lot about this technology. The most interesting and up-to-date blogs are:

- Jonathan Giles, who collects news and writes article about JavaFX at `http://fxexperience.com/`
- Michael Heinrichs, who gathers information from all over the world in his **JavaFX Daily** paper at `https://paper.li/net0pyr/1312275601#/`
- FxApps, which is focused on articles about various JavaFX applications at `http://fxapps.blogspot.ru/`

Future of JavaFX

Unfortunately, Oracle hasn't invest a lot into JavaFX lately. There were only a few new JavaFX features in Java 9, and almost none of them in Java 10. And, in Java 11, JavaFX is going to become a separate project, OpenJFX, which means it will not be included in the default Java 11 download.

Luckily, JavaFX is an open source project with an active community, which you can join and learn about at `https://wiki.openjdk.java.net/display/OpenJFX/Main`.

Summary

JavaFX is not just a set of APIs, it's a whole platform and ecosystem, as this chapter has shown. Over the course of this book, you've studied a large part of the JavaFX API and (I hope!) experimented with a lot of code samples.

We've made a long journey. We started from the scene creation, then filled it with shapes and basic controls, connected them together with Binding API, and styled through CSS and Effects. We learned the ways of FXML, and designed UI in SceneBuilder. To make our applications more dynamic, we used animation and various Layout Managers. We added video and audio through Media API, and presented web content through WebView. To deliver our apps to the end user we build it by javafxpackager and modularized with Jigsaw. And, in the end, we have drawn a few nice 3D samples.

That's a lot of information, but don't stop. Now you have all the instruments and can focus on your creativity to build beautiful and rich UI applications.

This is the last chapter, and I hope you've enjoyed the book and will build great UI with JavaFX in your projects.

Other Books You May Enjoy

If you enjoyed this book, you may be interested in these other books by Packt:

Hands-On GUI Programming with C++ and Qt5
Lee Zhi Eng

ISBN: 978-1-78839-782-7

- Implement tools provided by Qt 5 to design a beautiful GUI
- Understand different types of graphs and charts supported by Qt 5
- Create a web browser using the Qt 5 WebEngine module and web view widget
- Connect to the MySQL database and display data obtained from it onto the Qt 5 GUI
- Incorporate the Qt 5 multimedia and networking module in your application
- Develop Google Map-like applications using Qt 5's location module
- Discover cross-platform development by exporting the Qt 5 application to different platforms
- Uncover the secrets behind debugging Qt 5 and C++ applications

Tkinter GUI Application Development Blueprints - Second Edition
Bhaskar Chaudhary

ISBN: 978-1-78883-746-0

- A Practical, guide to help you learn the application of Python and GUI programming with Tkinter
- Create multiple, cross-platform, real-world projects by integrating a host of third-party libraries and tools
- Learn to build beautiful and highly interactive user interfaces, targeting multiple devices

Leave a review - let other readers know what you think

Please share your thoughts on this book with others by leaving a review on the site that you bought it from. If you purchased the book from Amazon, please leave us an honest review on this book's Amazon page. This is vital so that other potential readers can see and use your unbiased opinion to make purchasing decisions, we can understand what our customers think about our products, and our authors can see your feedback on the title that they have worked with Packt to create. It will only take a few minutes of your time, but is valuable to other potential customers, our authors, and Packt. Thank you!

Index

CPSIA information can be obtained
at www.ICGtesting.com
Printed in the USA
FSHW020126270720
72258FS

9 781788 293822